TORT LAW

Visit the *Law Express Series* Companion Website at
www.pearsoned.co.uk/lawexpress to find valuable **student**
learning material including:

- A Study Plan test to assess how well you know the subject
  before you begin your revision
- Interactive quizzes to test your knowledge of the main points
  from each chapter of the book
- Diagram plans for the questions in each chapter of the book
- Further examination questions and guidelines for answering
  them
- Interactive flashcards to help you revise the main cases
- Printable versions of the topic maps and checklists

TORT LAW

Emily Finch

Stefan Fafinski

PEARSON
Longman

Harlow, England • London • New York • Boston • San Francisco • Toronto • Sydney • Singapore • Hong Kong
Tokyo • Seoul • Taipei • New Delhi • Cape Town • Madrid • Mexico City • Amsterdam • Munich • Paris • Milan

Pearson Education Limited
Edinburgh Gate
Harlow
Essex CM20 2JE
England

and Associated Companies throughout the world

Visit us on the World Wide Web at:
www.pearsoned.co.uk

First published 2007

ISBN–13: 978-1-4058-2194-0
ISBN–10: 1-4058-2194-9

British Library Cataloguing-in-Publication Data
A catalogue record for this book is available from the British Library

Library of Congress Cataloging-in-Publication Data
A catalogue record for this book is available from the Library of Congress

10 9 8 7 6 5 4 3 2 1
11 10 09 08 07

Typeset by 3 in 10pt Helvetica Condensed
Printed by Ashford Colour Press Ltd., Gosport

The publisher's policy is to use paper manufactured from sustainable forests.

Contents

Acknowledgements   vii
Introduction   viii
Guided tour   x
Table of cases and statutes   xii

Chapter 1:   Negligence – duty of care and breach of duty   1
Chapter 2:   Negligence – causation and remoteness of
             damage   25
Chapter 3:   Special duties   39
Chapter 4:   Vicarious liability   54
Chapter 5:   Employers' liability   68
Chapter 6:   Occupiers' liability   82
Chapter 7:   Nuisance   96
Chapter 8:   Trespass to land   112
Chapter 9:   Trespass to the person   120
Chapter 10: Defamation   135
Chapter 11: Defences   147
Chapter 12: Remedies   162

Conclusion   175
Glossary of terms   178
Index   181

Supporting resources

Visit **www.pearsoned.co.uk/lawexpress** to find valuable online resources

Companion Website for students

- A Study Plan test to assess how well you know the subject before you begin your revision
- Interactive quizzes to test your knowledge of the main points from each chapter of the book
- Diagram plans for the questions in each chapter of the book
- Further examination questions and guidelines for answering them
- Interactive flashcards to help you revise the main cases
- Printable versions of the topic maps and checklists

Also: The Companion Website provides the following features:

- Search tool to help locate specific items of content
- E-mail results and profile tools to send results of quizzes to instructors
- Online help and support to assist with website usage and troubleshooting

For more information please contact your local Pearson Education sales representative or visit **www.pearsoned.co.uk/lawexpress**

Acknowledgements

The authors would like to thank everyone – academics and students alike – who has contributed towards the many reviews of drafts of this book for their comments, even where a good point has meant some major reworking. In particular we would like to thank Rebekah Taylor at Pearson Education for guiding us through the project and her endless patience during the process. Most importantly we would like to thank everyone at the Island Farm Donkey Sanctuary in Oxfordshire for providing us with a peaceful place to which to run away when necessary.

Stefan Fafinski
Emily Finch
March 2006

Introduction

Tort is one of the core subjects required for a qualifying law degree so it is a compulsory component of most undergraduate law programmes. It is usually taught as a first- or second-year subject as many of its concepts are relatively straightforward and it bears a certain resemblance to criminal law since it involves a similar two-stage process: the imposition of liability and the availability (or not) of a defence. Aspects of tort will appear in other subjects studied on the law degree: there are elements of negligence in employment law and environmental law whilst harassment is a prominent topic within family law. As such, it is important to have a strong grasp of tort both as a subject in its own right and because of the role it plays in many other law subjects.

Tort covers a wide range of issues that are pertinent to various aspects of everyday life such as the working environment, neighbour disputes and injuries sustained on another's premises. Negligence is a vast topic within tort that covers the many ways in which people inadvertently cause harm to each other. Due to the familiarity of many of the factual situations that arise in tort, students frequently feel quite comfortable with the subject. This can be a problem, however, if the situation gives rise to an outcome that seems unreasonable or unfair. It is important to remember to put aside instinctive evaluations of the situation and focus on the methodical application of the principles of law derived from case law and statute.

This revision guide will help you to identify the relevant law and apply it to factual situations which should help to overcome preconceived notions of the 'right' outcome in favour of legally accurate assessments of the liability of the parties. The book also provides guidance on the policy underlying the law and it identifies problem areas, both of which will help you to prepare for essay questions. The book is intended to supplement your course materials, lectures and textbooks; it is a guide to revision rather than a substitute for the amount of reading (and thinking) that you need to do in order to succeed. Tort is a vast subject – you should realise this from looking at the size of your recommended textbook – so it follows that a revision guide cannot cover all the depth and detail that you need to know and it does not set out to do so. Instead, it aims to provide a concise overall picture of the key areas for revision – reminding you of the headline points to enable you to focus your revision, and identify the key principles of law and the way to use these effectively in essays and problem questions.

REVISION NOTES

Things to bear in mind when revising tort law:

■ Do use this book to guide you through the revision process.

■ Do not use this book to tell you everything that you need to know about tort but make frequent reference to your recommended textbook and notes that you have made yourself from lectures and private study.

■ Make sure that you consult your syllabus frequently to check which topics are covered and in how much detail.

■ Read around the subject as much as possible to ensure that you have sufficient depth of knowledge. Use the suggested reading in this book and on your lecture handouts to help you to select relevant material.

■ Take every possible opportunity to practise your essay-writing and problem-solving technique; get as much feedback as you can.

■ You should aim to revise as much of the syllabus as possible. Be aware that many questions in tort that you encounter in coursework and examination papers will combine different topics, e.g. nuisance and trespass to land or employers' liability and trespass to the person. Equally, defences and/or remedies could combine with any of the torts. Therefore, selective revision could leave you unable to answer questions that include reference to material that you have excluded from your revision; it is never a good idea to tackle a question if you are only able to deal with part of the law that is raised.

Guided tour

Topic maps – Highlight the main points and allow you to find your way quickly and easily through each chapter.

2
Negligence – causation and remoteness of damage

Factual causation

Problems in proving factual causation

Multiple causes

Lost chances

Multiple consecutive causes

Causation

Novus actus interveniens

Third party act

Act of the claimant

Act of nature

Negligence – causation and remoteness

Remoteness

The test of remoteness

The egg shell skull rule

The impecunious claimant

Revision checklist – How well do you know each topic? Don't panic if you don't know them all, the chapters will help you to revise each point so that you will be fully prepared for your exams.

GLIGENCE – CAUSATION A

Revision Checklist

What you need to know:

☐ Explain factual causation and appl

☐ Identify and address the problems

☐ Appreciate the difficulties of esta

☐ The meaning of *novus actus in*

☐ The principles and policies

Sample questions – Prepare for what you will be faced with in your exams! Guidance on structuring strong answers is provided at the end of the chapter.

Problem question

Brenda dropped her grandson, Eddie, off at the bus station so that he could catch his bus home after he had come to visit for the weekend. She then went to her church meeting. Unfortunately, Eddie's bus had to swerve to avoid a lorry driven by Sid, who had fallen asleep at the wheel. The bus crashed into a petrol tanker and caught fire.
Brenda heard the next morning that Eddie had been on the bus and had died in the

Key definition boxes – Make sure you understand essential legal terms.

KEY DEFINITION

The organisation test makes a distinction between a *contract of service* whereby 'a man is employed as part of the business and his work is done as an integral part of the business' and a *contract for services* whereby 'work, although done for the business, is not integrated into it but is only accessory to it': *Stevenson, Jordan and Harrison Ltd* v. *Macdonald and Evans* [1952] 1 TLR 101.

Newstead v. London Express Newpaper Ltd [1940] 1 KB 377

Concerning: mis-identification of claimant

Facts

The defendant newspaper reported that Harold Newstead, aged 30 of Camberwell, was convicted of bigamy. Although this was true, another Harold Newstead from Camberwell of that age brought an action for libel on the basis that it was untrue (and defamatory) in relation to him.

Legal principle

It was held that the statement was defamatory as the reasonable person would think that the statement referred to the claimant.

Key case and key statutory provision boxes – Identify the essential cases and statutes that you need to know for your exams.

Defamation Act 1996, section 2

Provides that the publisher of a defamatory statement may make amends and thus avoid liability if he:

▌ Makes a suitable correction and apology
▌ Publishes these in a reasonable manner
▌ Pays compensation to the claimant.

Further thinking boxes – Illustrate areas of academic debate, and point you towards that extra reading required for the top grades.

FURTHER THINKING

The test formulated in *Lister* has implications for vicarious liability in that it imposed liability on an 'innocent' employer for the intentional criminal acts of an employee. You might find it useful to read the House of Lords decision for insight into the policy underlying the decision. The following article also provides a detailed analysis of the decision and would make useful reading in preparation for an essay:

Roe, R., 'Lister v. Henley Hall' (2002) *Modern Law Review* vol. 65, 270

Glossary – Forgotten the meaning of a word? – Where a word is highlighted in the text, turn to the glossary at the back of the book to remind yourself of its meaning.

Glossary of terms

Key definitions

Assault	'An act which causes another person to apprehend the infliction of immediate, unlawful force on his person: *Collins* v. *Wilcox* [1984] 3 All ER 374 *per* Lord Goff
Battery	'The intentional and direct application of force to another person' (Rogers, W.V.H. (2002) *Winfield and Jolowicz on Tort*, 16th edn, London: Sweet & Maxwell, p. 71)
Consent	A defence which is frequently referred to by the Latin term *volenti non fit injuria*. The literal translation of this is 'there can be no injury to one who consents' although it is often said to mean 'voluntary assumption of risk'

Exam tips – Want to impress examiners? These indicate how you can improve your exam performance and your chances of getting top marks.

EXAM TIP

No one test is accepted as authoritative by the courts although it is the economic reality test that tends to be applied as it covers aspects of both of the other tests. In any essay, you might want to consider how these tests have evolved and address whether they provide a reliable means for distinguishing employees and independent contractors. In a problem question, you will need to apply the economic reality test to determine whether someone is an employee, remembering to take into account the factors listed above in deciding the third limb of the *Ready Mixed Concrete* test.

Revision notes – Highlight points that you should be aware of in other topic areas, or where your own course may adopt a specific approach that you should check with your course tutor before reading further.

REVISION NOTE

It is often the case that the relevant tort is negligence so make sure that you have a good grasp of this topic. However, vicarious liability can apply to any tort so it might be useful to remind yourself of the key principles of the various torts that you have studied and think about how these could occur in an employer/employee relationship.

Table of cases and statutes

Cases

A v. *B plc* [2002] 2 All ER 504 144

A v. *UK* [1998] Fam LR 118 127

AG Securities v. *Vaughan* [1988] 3 All ER 1058 117

Adams v. *Rhymney Valley DC* [2000] Lloyd's Rep PN 777 13

Alcock v. *Chief Constable of South Yorkshire* [1992] 4 All ER 907 48–50, 52

American Cyanamid v. *Ethicon* [1975] AC 396 171

Anns v. *Merton London Borough Council* [1978] AC 728 40, 43, 44, 176

Attia v. *British Gas plc* [1987] 3 All ER 455 50

Attorney-General v. *PYA Quarries Ltd* [1957] 2 QB 169 104, 105, 179

Baker v. *TE Hopkins & Son Ltd* [1959] 3 All ER 225 157

Baker v. *Willoughby* [1969] 3 All ER 1528 32

Barkway v. *South Wales Transport* [1950] 1 All ER 392 20

Barnett v. *Chelsea and Kensington Hospital Management Committee* [1969] 1 QB 428 28

Barrett v. *Enfield London Borough Council* [1999] 3 All ER 193 10

Beard v. *London Omnibus Co* [1990] 2 QB 530 62

Berkoff v. *Birchell* [1996] 4 All ER 1008 139

Bernstein v. *Skyviews and General Ltd* [1977] 2 All ER 902 117

Bird v. *Jones* (1845) 7 QB 742 129

Blyth v. *Birmingham Waterworks* (1856) 11 Exch 781 11, 12, 23

Bolam v. *Friern Hospital Manangement Committee* [1957] 2 All ER 118 13, 23

Bolitho v. *City and Hackney Health Authority* [1997] 4 All ER 771 14, 23

Bolton v. *Stone* [1951] AC 850 17

Bonnington Castings Ltd v. *Wardlaw* [1956] AC 613 29, 30, 78

Brice v. *Brown* [1984] 1 All ER 997 51, 52

Brown v. *NCB* [1962] AC 574 77

Burton v. *Islington Health Authority* [1922] 3 All ER 833 9

Bux v. *Slough Metals* [1974] 1 All ER 262 73, 80

Byrne v. *Deane* [1937] 2 All ER 204 139

Calgrath, The [1927] P 93 86

Camarthenshire County Council v. *Lewis* [1955] AC 549 8

Candler v. *Crane Christmas & Co* [1951] 2 KB 533 44

Caparo Industries plc v. *Dickman* [1990] 1 All ER 568 6, 7, 23, 46

Capital and Counties plc v. *Hampshire County Council* [1997] QB 1004 10

Carslogie Steamship Co Ltd v. *Royal Norweigan Government* [1952] AC 292 34

Casidy v. *Daily Mirror Group Newspapers Ltd* [1929] 2 KB 331 140

Cassidy v. *Ministry of Health* [1951] 2 KB 343 21

Castle v. *St Augustine's Links* (1922) 38 TLR 615 105

Caswell v. *Powell Duffryn Associated Collieries Ltd* [1940] AC 152 79, 80

Century Insurance v. *NI Road Transport Board* [1942] AC 509 61, 62

Chadwick v. *British Railways Board* [1967] 2 All ER 945 47

Chaudry v. *Prabhakar* [1989] 1 WLR 29 46

Christie v. *Davey* [1893] 1 Ch 316 103

Cole v. *Turner* (1704) 6 Mod Rep 149 124

Collins v. *Wilcox* [1984] 3 All ER 374 124, 178

Conway v. *George Wimpey & Co* [1951] 2 KB 266 115

Cook v. *Square D Ltd* [1992] ACR 262 71

Cork v. *Kirby MacLean Ltd* [1952] 2 All ER 402 27

Cornish v. *Midland Bank plc* [1985] 3 All ER 513 46

Cummings v. *Granger* [1977] 1 All ER 104 153

Cutler v. *Wandsworth Stadium Ltd* [1949] AC 398 76, 80

D & F Estates Ltd v. *Church Commissioners for England* [1989] AC 177 44

Darbon v. *Bath Tramways Mtor Co Ltd* [1946] 2 All ER 333 19

Donoghue v. *Stevenson* [1932] AC 562 5–7, 23

Donovan v. *The Face* (1992) unreported 140

Dooley v. *Cammell Laird and Co Ltd* [1951] 1 Lloyd's Rep 271 49

Easson v. *LNER* [1944] 2 KB 421 20

East Suffolk River Catchment Board v. *Kent and Another* [1940] 1 All ER 527 6

F, Re [1999] 2 AC 1 128

F v. *West Berkshire HA* [1989] 2 All ER 545 124

Fardon v. *Harcourt-Rivington* [1932] All ER 81 19

Fairchild v. *Glenhaven Funeral Services Ltd* [2003] 3 WLR 89 30

Fosbroke-Hobbes v. *Airwork Ltd* [1937] 1 All ER 108 86

Froom v. *Butcher* [1975] 3 All ER 520 158, 161

General Cleaning Contractors v. *Christmas* [1953] AC 180 71

Gillick v. *West Norfolk and Wisbech AHA* [1986] AC 112 151

Glasgow Corporation v. *Taylor* [1922] 1 AC 44 89

Gorely v. *Codd* [1967] 1 WLR 19 15

Gorris v. *Scott* (1874) LR 9 Exch 125 78, 80

Gough v. *Thorne* [1966] 3 All ER 398 156

Groves v. *Lord Wimborne* [1898] All ER Rep 147 76

Haley v. *London Electricity Board* [1964] 3 All ER 185 17

Hall v. *Brooklands Auto-Racing Club* [1933] 1 KB 205 12

Harris v. *Birkenhead Corporation* [1976] 1 All ER 341 85

Harrison v. *Vincent* [1982] RTR 8 16

Hartley v. *Mayoh & Co* [1954] 1 QB 383 76, 80

Hasledine v. *Daw & Son Ltd* [1941] 3 All ER 156 92

Hay or Bourhill v. *Young* [1942] 2 All ER 396 47

Hedley Byrne v. *Heller and Partners Ltd* [1964] AC 465 45, 46

Hill v. *Chief Constable of West Yorkshire* [1989] AC 53 9

Hollywood Silver Fox Farm Ltd v. *Emmett* [1936] 2 KB 468 103

Home Office v. *Dorset Yacht Co Ltd* [1970] AC 1004 7

Hotson v. *East Berkshire Area Health Authority* [1987] 2 All ER 909 30

Hudson v. *Ridge Manufacturing Co.* [1957] 2 QB 348 8

Hunter v. *British Coal* [1998] 2 All ER 97 50

Hunter v. *Canary Wharf* [1997] 2 All ER 426 100, 104, 105

ICI Ltd v. *Shatwell* [1964] 2 All ER 999 79

Iqbal v. *London Transport Executive* (1973) 16 KIR 329 62

Jobling v. *Associated Daries Ltd* [1982] 2 All ER 752 32, 33

Joel v. *Morrison* (1834) 6 C & P 501 60, 179

John v. *Mirror Group Newspapers* [1996] 2 All ER 35 143

John Summers & Sons Ltd v. *Frost* [1955] AC 740 77, 80

Jones v. *Boyce* (1816) 1 Stark 492 157

Jones v. *Livox Quarries* [1952] 2 QB 608 155

Jones v. *Manchester Corporation* [1952] 2 All ER 125 65

Junior Books Ltd v. *Veitchi Co Ltd* [1983] 1 AC 520 40, 43, 44, 176

Kennaway v. *Thompson* [1981] QB 88 110

Kent v. *Griffiths, Roberts and London Ambulance Service* [1998] EWCA Civ 1941 10

Khorasandjian v. *Bush* [1993] 3 WLR 476 100

Knightley v. *Johns* [1982] 1 All ER 851 32

Knowles v. *Liverpool County Council* [1994] 1 Lloyd's Rep 11 72, 80

Knuppfer v. *London Express Newspapers* [1944] 1 All ER 495 141

Kralj v. *McGrath* [1986] 1 All ER 54 47

Lamb v. *Camden London Borough Council* [1981] QB 625 32

Latimer v. *AEC Ltd* [1953] AC 643 18, 71, 80

Leach v. *Chief Constable of Gloucestershire Constabulary* [1999] 1 All ER 215 47, 52

Letang v. *Cooper* [1964] 2 All ER 929 123

Liesbosch Dredger v. *SS Edison* [1933] AC 449 37

Lister v. *Romford Ice & Cold Storage Co Ltd* [1957] 1 All ER 125 65

Lister and others v. *Helsey Hall Ltd* [2001] 2 All ER 769 63, 64, 67

Livingstone v. *MoD* [1984] NI 356 123

Lloyd v. *Green Smith & Co* [1912] AC 716 64

London County Council v. *Cattermoles (Garages) Ltd* [1953] 1 WLR 997 62

London Graving Dock v. *Horton* [1951] AC 737 85

Lonrho Ltd v. *Shell Petroleum Co Ltd (No 2)* [1982] AC 173 75

Lowery v. *Walker* [1911] AC 10 87

Luxmoore-May v. *Messenger May Baverstock* [1990] 1 WLR 1009 13

McFarlane v. *EE Caledonia Ltd* [1995] 1 Lloyd's Rep 535 50

McGhee v. *National Coal Board* [1973] 3 All ER 1008 30

McKew v. *Holland & Hannen & Cubitts (Scotland) Ltd* [1969] 3 All ER 1621 33

McLoughlin v. *O'Brian* [1982] 2 All ER 298 50, 52

McWilliams v. *Sir William Arrol & Co Ltd* [1962] 1 WLR 295 72

Malone v. *Laskey* [1907] 2 QB 141 100

Mattocks v. *Mann* [1993] RTR 13 37

Miller v. *Jackson* [1977] QB 966; [1977] 3 All ER 338 17, 98, 179

Morales v. *Eccleston* [1991] RTR 151 156

Morgan v. *Odhams Press* [1971] 1 WLR 1239 140, 141

Morris v. *Murray* [1990] 3 All ER 801 150

Mullins v. *Richards* [1998] 1 All ER 920 15

Murphy v. *Brentwood District Council* [1990] 2 All ER 908 40, 44, 176

Murphy v. *Culhane* [1977] QB 74 153

Murray v. *Ministry of Defence* [1988] 2 All ER 521 129

Nettleship v. *Weston* [1971] 3 All ER 581 14, 23, 38

Newstead v. *London Express Newspaper Ltd* [1940] 1 KB 377 140

Ng Chun Pui v. *Lee Cheun Tat* [1988] RTR 298 21

OLL Ltd v. *Secretary of State for Transport* [1997] 3 All ER 397 10

Overseas Tankship (UK) Ltd v. *Morts Dock and Engineering Co Ltd (The Wagon Mound) (No 1)* [1961] 1 All ER 404 35, 36, 38, 107

Osman v. UK [1991] 1 FLR 193 10

Page v. Smith [1995] 2 All ER 736 49, 52

Pape v. Cumbria County Council [1992] 3 All ER 211 73

Paris v. Stepney Borough Council [1951] AC 367 18

Parmiter v. Coupland (1840) 6 M & W 105 139, 178

Performance Cars Ltd v. Abraham [1962] 1 QB 33 31

Perry v. Sidney Phillips [1982] All ER 705 37

Phipps v. Rochester Corporation [1955] 1 QB 450 89

Polemis and Furness, Re; Withy & Co Ltd [1921] 3 KB 560 34–36

Pursell v. Horn (1838) 8 A & E 602 123

R v. George (1840) 9 C & P 483 126

R v. Ireland [1997] 4 All ER 225 125

R v. Johnson [1997] 1 WLR 367 105, 106

R v. Lowrie [2005] 1 Cr App R 530 106

R v. Meade and Belt (1823) 1 Lew CC 184 124

R v. Ony [2001] 1 Cr App R (S) 404 105

R v. Rimmington [2005] UKHL 63 106

R v. Ruffell (1991) 13 Cr App R (S) 204 105

Rahman v. Arearose Ltd [2000] 3 WLR 1184 73

Rantzen v. Mirror Group Newspapers [1994] QB 670 143

Ready Mixed Concrete Ltd v. Minister of Pensions [1968] 2 QB 497 59, 60

Redland Bricks Ltd v. Morris [1970] AC 652 169

Revill v. Newbury [1996] 1 All ER 291 127, 153

Reynolds v. Times Newspapers [2001] 2 AC 127 142

Robert Addie & Sons (Collieries) Ltd v. Dumbreck [1929] AC 358 93, 180

Robinson v. Kilvert (1889) 41 Ch D 88 102

Rookes v. Barnard [1964] AC 1129 168, 174

Scott v. London & St Katherine Docks Co (1865) 3 H & C 596 20, 21

Scott v. Shepherd (1773) 2 BIR 892 123

Sidaway v. Bethlem Royal & Maudsley Hospital Governors [1985] 1 All ER 643 13

Silkin v. Beaverbrook Newspapers [1958] 1 WLR 743 142

Sim v. Stretch (1936) 52 TLR 669 139, 178

Smith v. Baker [1891] AC 325 151

Smith v. Leech Brain & Co Ltd [1961] 3 All ER 1159 36

Smith v. Littlewoods Organisation Ltd [1987] 2 WLR 480 8

Smith v. Stone (1647) Style 65 115

Smoldon v. Whitworth and Nolan [1997] PIQR 133 16, 152

Spartan Steel and Alloys Ltd v. Martin & Co (Contractors) Ltd [1973] 1 QB 27 42

Speed v. Thomas Swift & Co Ltd [1943] 1 KB 557 73, 80

Spring v. Guardian Assurance plc [1994] 2 WLR 354 46

St Helen's Smelting Co v. Tippings (1865) 11 HL Cas 642 101

Staples v. West Dorset District Council [1995] 93 LGR 536 90

Stapley v. Gypsum Mines Ltd [1953] 2 All ER 478 157

Stevenson, Jordan and Harrison Ltd v. Macdonald and Evans [1952] 1 TLR 101 58, 179

Storey v. Ashton (1869) LR 4 QB 476 60

Sturges v. Bridgeman (1879) 11 Ch D 852 101, 108

Sutcliffe v. Pressdram [1991] 1 QB 153 143

Thomas v. National Union of Mineworkers [1985] 2 All ER 1 126

Thompson v. Metropolitan Police Commissioners [1997] 2 All ER 762 167

Titchener v. BRB [1983] 3 All ER 770 89

Tolley v. Fry & Sons Ltd [1931] AC 331 140

Vellino v. Chief Constable of Greater

Manchester Police [2002] 3 All ER 78 153

Vernon v. *Bosley (No. 1)* [1997] 1 All ER 577 47, 52

Walker v. *Northumberland County Council* [1995] 1 All ER 737 73

Walton v. *North Cornwall District Council* [1997] 1 WLR 570 46

Ward v. *Tesco Stores Ltd* [1976] 1 WLR 810 21

Watt v. *Hertfordshire County Council* [1954] 1 WLR 835 19

Wells v. *Cooper* [1958] 2 QB 265 15

Wheat v. *E Lacon & Co Ltd* [1966] 1 All ER 582 85, 179

Wheeler v. *Copas* [1981] 3 All ER 405 86

Wheeler v. *JJ Saunders Ltd* [1996] Ch 19 108

Wheeler v. *New Merton Board Mills Ltd* [1933] 2 KB 669 79, 80

White v. *Jones* [1995] 1 All ER 691 46

White and Others v. *Chief Constable of the South Yorkshire Police* [1999] 1 All ER 1 49, 51, 52

Wigg v. *British Railways Board* (1986) 136 NLJ 446 49

Wilkinson v. *Downton* [1897] 2 QB 57 122, 130, 131, 133, 134

Wilsher v. *Essex Area Health Authority* [1988] 1 All ER 871, HL; *affirming* [1986] 3 All ER 801 15, 29, 30

Wilson & Clyde Coal Co Ltd v. *English* [1937] 3 All ER 628 70, 80

Wong v. *Parkside NHS Trust* [2001] EWCA Civ 1721 130, 133

Woodward v. *Mayor of Hastings* [1945] 1 KB 174 92

Wooldridge v. *Sumner* [1963] 2 QB 43; [1962] 2 All ER 978 16, 152

X (Minors) v. *Bedfordshire County Council* [1995] 3 All ER 353 10

Yachuk v. *Oliver Blais* [1949] AC 386 156

Yewen v. *Noakes* (1880) 6 QBD 530 57, 178

Z v. *UK* [2002] 34 EHRR 3 10

Statutes

Cable and Broadcasting Act 1984 138
Civil Aviation Act 1982 108
Civil Evidence Act 1968 21
s 11 19, 21, 23
Civil Liability (Contribution) Act 1978 54, 64
s 1(1) 64
s 2(1) 65
Congenital Disabilities (Civil Liability) Act 1976 9
Consumer Protection Act 1987 75
Contagious Diseases (Animals) Act 1869
s 75 78
Courts and Legal Services Act 1990 143
Defamation Act 1952
s 1 138
s 5 142
Defamation Act 1996
s 1 141
s 2 143
Employers' Liability (Defective Equipment) Act 1969 72
s 1(1)(b) 72
Factories Act 1961 80
s 14(1) 70, 77, 80
Factory and Workshop Act 1901 76
Factory and Workshop Act 1907 76
Factory and Workshop Act 1908 76
Health and Safety at Work Act 1974 69, 74
Human Rights Act 1998 136
Law Reform (Contributory Negligence) Act 1945 92
s 1(1) 154
s 4 154
Limitation Act 1980
s 4A 138
Malicious Communications Act 1988
s 1 106
Mental Health Act 1983 126, 130
Mineral Workings (Offshore Installations) Act 1971 75
Misrepresentation Act 1967 75
National Parks and Access to the Countryside Act 1949

s 60 92
Occupiers' Liability Act 1957 83, 84, 92,
    94, 176
s 1(1) 85
s 2(1) 88
s 2(2) 87
s 2(3)(a) 88
s 2(3)(b) 88, 90
s 2(4)(a) 90
s 2(4)(b) 91
s 2(5) 92
s 3(1)(a) 85
Occupiers' Liability Act 1984 83, 84, 86,
    92, 176
s 1(1) 92
s 1(3) 93
Police and Criminal Evidence Act 1984
    118, 126, 128, 130
Protection from Harassment Act 1997
    100, 131
s 1 131, 132
s 1(2) 132
s 3 131
s 7(2) 132
s 7(3) 132
s 7(4) 132
Public Health (Control of Disease) Act
    1984 130
Road Traffic Act 1998

s 3 22
s 149(3) 151
Serious Organised Crime and Police Act
    2005
s 110 128
Southern Rhodesia Act 1965 75
Supreme Court Act 1981
s 69 138
Theatres Act 1968 138

Statutory Instruments

Grinding of Metals (Miscellaneous
    Industries) Regulations 1925, SI
    1925/904 78

European Legislation

European Convention on the Protection
    of Human Rights and Fundamental
    Freedoms
Art 3 127
Art 5 121
Art 6 121
Art 8 121, 136
Art 10 121, 136

1

Negligence – duty of care and breach of duty

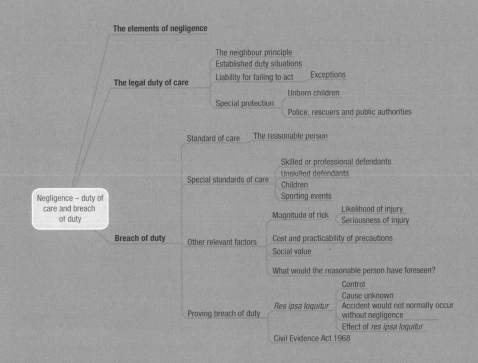

The elements of negligence

The legal duty of care
- The neighbour principle
- Established duty situations
- Liability for failing to act — Exceptions
- Special protection
  - Unborn children
  - Police, rescuers and public authorities

Negligence – duty of care and breach of duty

Breach of duty

Standard of care — The reasonable person

Special standards of care
- Skilled or professional defendants
- Unskilled defendants
- Children
- Sporting events

Other relevant factors
- Magnitude of risk
  - Likelihood of injury
  - Seriousness of injury
- Cost and practicability of precautions
- Social value
- What would the reasonable person have foreseen?

Proving breach of duty
- Res ipsa loquitur
  - Control
  - Cause unknown
  - Accident would not normally occur without negligence
  - Effect of res ipsa loquitur
- Civil Evidence Act 1968

Revision checklist

What you need to know:

- [ ] The composite elements required to establish negligence
- [ ] The definition of the legal duty of care
- [ ] Established and special duty of care situations
- [ ] General and special standards of care
- [ ] How to determine the standard of care and prove breach of duty.

Introduction
Negligence

Negligence has grown to become the largest area of tort law.

In everyday terms, negligence means failure to pay attention to what ought to be done or to take the required level of care. Its everyday usage implies a state of mind (carelessness) whereas the tort of negligence is concerned with the link between the defendant's behaviour and the risk that ought to have been foreseen. When revising negligence, be careful not to let the everyday meaning of the word distract you from the legal meaning of negligence.

As negligence is such an immense topic, it has been broken down into two chapters in this book. It may help to think of this chapter as dealing with the question of whether or not the defendant's conduct is negligent (duty of care and breach of that duty) whilst the next chapter considers whether that negligent conduct caused the harm suffered by the claimant (causation and remoteness).

Essay question advice

Essays on negligence are common. As you will see in the coming chapters, many aspects of this tort have been scrutinised by the courts so there is plenty of scope for an essay question on the issues that have received judicial scrutiny. As the topic is so immense, essays that focus on negligence as a whole are unlikely. Just as these chapters break negligence into segments, essays are likely to pick a particular element of negligence as a focus.

Problem question advice

When attacking a problem question on negligence it is important to be systematic in your approach. If you are trying to establish negligence, start by defining it and listing out the elements of the tort, before dealing with each element in turn. This will lead to a well-structured argument that should be easier for the marker to follow. Remember to cover each element, even if the facts of the case make it unproblematic or obvious. Every element of the tort must be present and discussed in your answer – missing out the straightforward parts will lose you valuable and easy marks as a result. Don't forget to substantiate each of the points you make with relevant case law.

Sample question

Could you answer this question? Below is a typical problem question that could arise on this topic. Guidelines on answering the first part of the question are included at the end of the chapter. These will cover duty of care and breach of duty. Causation and remoteness will be dealt with in the next chapter, when we return to the same question. A sample essay question and guidance on tackling it can be found on the companion website.

Problem question

The Henley Donkey Sanctuary sends donkeys out each year to Palm Sunday services. Roy, the vicar of St Raymond's, arrived to pick up Princess (a placid, if occasionally stubborn donkey) with his car and trailer. Before setting off back to the church, Roy failed to check that the trailer was properly coupled to the lorry. On the way back, while going uphill, the trailer became unhitched and rolled back down the hill. It hit Wayne, who was riding his new Lambretta. Wayne was just wearing a tracksuit, rather than leathers or a helmet. His scooter was destroyed and he was taken to hospital. Chelsea, who was out on her first driving lesson, tried to brake to avoid the trailer, but hit the accelerator instead, driving off the road and into a tree, causing £4000 damage to her instructor's car and causing him a severe whiplash injury. The trailer came to a gentle stop outside Flo's house. Princess, who was unharmed, pushed open the trailer door (the lock had broken on its descent) and calmed herself down by eating Flo's crop of marrows which she had hoped to enter into the local vegetable show that year since there was a £1000 prize on offer for the best marrow, and Flo was confident of victory.

Wayne was taken to hospital, where Dr Roberts, a junior doctor on his second day, examined Wayne's x-rays, decided that there was nothing wrong with him and sent him home. That night, Wayne developed a blood clot on his lung and died. Expert medical opinion was divided as to whether the results of Wayne's x-rays merited treatment at the hospital, although it was discovered that Wayne had a rare undiagnosed blood disorder that made him much more susceptible to developing potentially fatal clots.

Roy was subsequently convicted of careless driving.

Discuss the various claims in negligence that may arise on these facts.

■The elements of negligence

> **KEY DEFINITION**
>
> **Negligence** as a tort is a breach of legal duty to take care which results in damage to the claimant. (Rogers, W.V.H. (2002) *Winfield and Jolowicz on Tort*, 16th edn, London: Sweet & Maxwell, p. 103)

This definition of negligence can be broken down into the four component parts that a claimant must prove to establish negligence. The legal burden of proving each of these elements falls upon the claimant. See Figure 1.1.

Figure 1.1

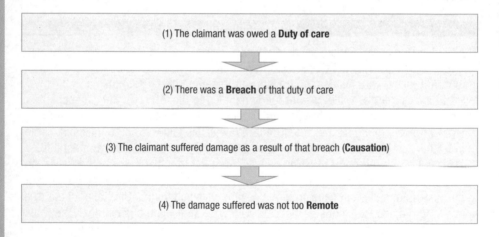

(1) The claimant was owed a **Duty of care**

(2) There was a **Breach** of that duty of care

(3) The claimant suffered damage as a result of that breach (**Causation**)

(4) The damage suffered was not too **Remote**

■Duty of care

The first element of negligence is the legal duty of care. This concerns the relationship between the defendant and claimant, which must be such that there is an obligation upon the defendant to take proper care to avoid causing injury to the claimant in all the circumstances of the case.

There are two ways in which a duty of care may be established:

■ The defendant and claimant are within one of the 'special relationships'; or
■ Outside of these relationships, according to the principles developed by case law.

Established duty situations

There are a number of situations in which the courts recognise the existence of a duty of care. These usually arise as a result of some sort of special relationship between the parties. Examples include:

■ One road-user to another
■ Employer to employee
■ Manufacturer to consumer (see *Donoghue* v. *Stevenson*)
■ Doctor to patient
■ Solicitor to client.

The neighbour principle

Outside of these categories of established duty, a duty of care will be determined on the basis of individual circumstances. The 'neighbour principle' formulated by Lord Atkin in *Donoghue* v. *Stevenson* [1932] AC 562 was initially used to determine whether a duty of care existed between defendant and claimant:

KEY CASE

Donoghue v. *Stevenson* [1932] AC 562

Concerning: duty of care; neighbour principle

Facts

Mrs Donoghue and a friend visited a café. Mrs Donoghue's friend bought her a bottle of ginger beer. The bottle was made of opaque glass. When filling Mrs Donoghue's glass, the remains of a decomposed snail – which had somehow found its way into the bottle at the factory – floated out. Mrs Donoghue developed gastroenteritis as a result.

Legal principle

Since Mrs Donoghue had not bought the bottle of ginger beer herself she could not make a claim in contract upon breach of warranty. She therefore brought an action against the manufacturer of the ginger beer. The House of Lords had to decide whether a duty of care existed as a matter of law.

The House of Lords held that the manufacturer owed her a duty to take care that the bottle did not contain foreign bodies which could cause her

▶

KEY CASE

personal harm. This is known as the *narrow rule* in *Donoghue* v. *Stevenson* – that a manufacturer of goods owes a duty of care to their ultimate consumer.

More importantly, the case establishes the *neighbour principle* which determines whether the defendant owes a duty of care in any situation. Lord Atkin stated:

> You must take reasonable care to avoid acts or omissions which you can reasonably foresee would be likely to injure your neighbour. Who, then, in law is my neighbour? The answer seems to be persons who are so closely and directly affected by my act that I ought reasonably to have them in my contemplation as being so affected when I am directing my mind to the acts or omissions which are called in question.

The neighbour principle is not limited in its application. As Lord Macmillan said in *Donoghue* v. *Stevenson*: 'The categories of negligence are never closed'. This means that the courts can formulate new categories of negligence to reflect the current social view and make decisions based on consideration of public policy.

The basic concept of the neighbour principle was reconsidered more recently in *Caparo Industries plc* v. *Dickman* [1990] 1 All ER 568.

KEY CASE

Caparo Industries plc v. *Dickman* [1990] 1 All ER 568

Concerning: duty of care

Facts

The case considered the liability of an auditor for financial loss suffered by investors. However, it also set out the three points which a court must consider to establish whether a duty of care exists.

Legal principle

The three points are:

- Reasonable foresight of harm
- Sufficient proximity of relationship
- That it is fair, just and reasonable to impose a duty.

Caparo v. *Dickman* effectively redefined the neighbour principle such that it adds the requirement that there must be a relationship of sufficient proximity and that the imposition of a duty of care must be fair, just and reasonable. The comparison can be seen in the following table:

Caparo v. *Dickman*	*Donoghue* v. *Stevenson*
Reasonable foresight of harm	Avoid acts or omissions which you can reasonably foresee would be likely to injure your neighbour
Sufficient proximity of relationship	Persons who are so closely and directly affected by my act that I ought reasonably to have them in my contemplation as being so affected when I am directing my mind to the acts or omissions which are called in question
Fair, just and reasonable to impose a duty	

EXAM TIP

When discussing the duty of care in your answers it is important to remember the third requirement imposed by *Caparo* v. *Dickman*.

The basic elements that need to be considered in establishing duty of care are illustrated in Figure 1.2.

Liability for failing to act

In general, you do not owe a duty to the world to take positive action to prevent harm. If you see someone in peril, you are not obliged to try to rescue them, and if you fail to do so you cannot be liable in negligence for not acting positively. So, if you see a stranger face down in a pond, you do not have any legal obligation to prevent them from drowning – even though you might feel a strong *moral* obligation to do so.

If you *do* intervene, however, you are still not liable in negligence, unless you make matters worse (*East Suffolk Rivers Catchment Board* v. *Kent and another* [1940] 1 All ER 527).

Exceptions

There is a duty to act positively if there is a special relationship or a relationship of power or control between the parties. Examples include:

▪ Prison officers and prisoners (*Home Office* v. *Dorset Yacht Co. Ltd* [1970] AC 1004)

Figure 1.2

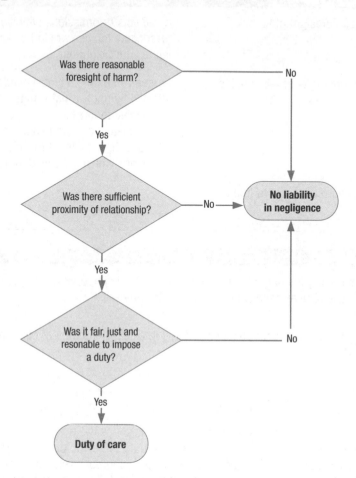

■ Employer and employee (*Hudson* v. *Ridge Manufacturing Co.* [1957] 2 QB 348)
■ Occupier and visitor (see Chapter 6 on occupiers' liability)
■ Parent and child (*Carmarthenshire County Council* v. *Lewis* 1955] AC 549).

EXAM TIP

If you are faced with a problem question in which someone fails to act and loss or damage results, you should be careful to establish whether or not a special relationship exists. A good rule of thumb is whether it seems reasonable for the party in question to act. While there is no obligation to prevent a stranger from drowning in a pond, the situation would be quite different in the case of a parent who watched their child drown in a paddling pool and did nothing.

Special protection

The law of negligence has no statutory basis. It has developed through a huge number of cases. This has meant that when considering whether a duty of care exists in any given situation, the courts have the flexibility to take public policy considerations into account and steer the evolution of the tort of negligence accordingly. This flexibility has also allowed the courts to protect certain classes of defendant from liability in negligence and also to provide additional help to certain classes of claimant in bringing an action.

Unborn children

The existence of a duty of care requires reasonable foresight of harm. However, in the case of unborn children, the defendant might not realise that the female claimant is pregnant, although it is quite possible that a person's negligence might harm an unborn child.

In *Burton* v. *Islington Health Authority* [1992] 3 All ER 833 it was held that a duty of care is owed to an unborn child which becomes actionable on birth. In other words, a child can sue in negligence for events occurring during its time in its mother's womb. This common law position is only applicable to persons born prior to 22 July 1976 when the Congenital Disabilities (Civil Liability) Act 1976 came into force. This Act gives a right of action to a child who is born alive and disabled in respect of the disability, if it is caused by an occurrence which affected the mother during pregnancy or the mother or child during labour, causing disabilities which would not otherwise have been present. It extends to pre-conception torts, where the mother is harmed prior to conceiving and the harm suffered affects the health of the baby at birth.

Police, rescuers and public authorities

The courts have found that there is no general duty of care owed by the *police* to any particular individual. In *Hill* v. *Chief Constable of West Yorkshire* [1989] AC 53 it was held that the duty of the police is to the public *at large*.

This approach has been extended to cases involving the *fire service* (*Capital and Counties plc* v. *Hampshire County Council* [1997] QB 1004) and the *coastguard* (*OLL Ltd* v. *Secretary of State for Transport* [1997] 3 All ER 397). In respect of the *ambulance service* there is no general duty to respond to a call, although once a call has been accepted, the service owes a duty to the named individual at a specific address (*Kent* v. *Griffiths, Roberts and London Ambulance Service* [1998] EWCA Civ 1941) provided that it is just, fair and reasonable to impose such a duty.

In respect of *public authorities*, it was held in *X (Minors)* v. *Bedfordshire County*

Council [1995] 3 All ER 353, that in most instances an action in negligence against a public authority carrying out its delegated powers would fail.

○ REVISION NOTE

You may have covered the remedies available under judicial review where a public body acts beyond its authority (*ultra vires*) in constitutional and administrative law. If so, it might be useful to refresh your memory as to how local authorities operate under powers delegated from the executive.

However, in *Barrett* v. *Enfield London Borough Council* [1999] 3 All ER 193, Lord Hutton disagreed with the decision in *X* v. *Bedfordshire County Council*, considering that challenges based upon the careless exercise of discretionary powers by a public authority *could* be founded in negligence.

In both cases, though, the House of Lords was careful to limit the possible liability of public authorities in negligence. If every decision they made was potentially actionable in tort, this would impose unworkable restraints on their ability to perform their functions and be contrary to public interest. The courts will attempt to balance the social need for the public authority to carry out its duties effectively and the need for an adequate remedy for the individual who suffers from the negligent exercise of the public authority's discretion.

This partial immunity has been subject to appeal in the European Court of Human Rights. In *Osman* v. *UK* [1999] 1 FLR 193, the ECtHR held that police immunity violated the Article 6 right to a fair hearing. In *Z* v. *UK* (2002) 34 EHRR 3 the ECtHR held that the immunity applied in X subjected the claimants to 'inhuman and degrading treatment' (Article 3) and denied them an effective remedy (Article 13).

■ Breach of duty

The second element of negligence is *breach of duty*. Having established that a duty of care exists in law and in the particular situation, the next step in establishing liability is to decide whether the defendant is in breach of that duty – in other words, whether the defendant has not come up to the *standard of care* required by law. See Figure 1.3.

Figure 1.3

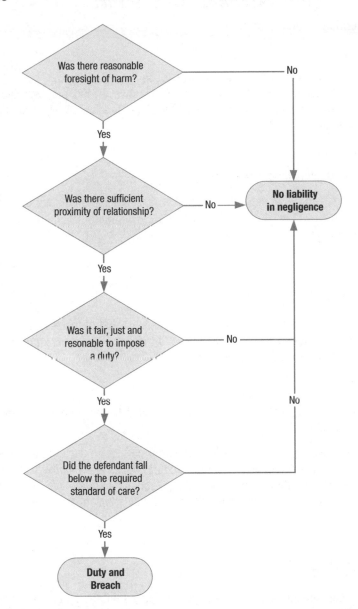

Standard of care

The standard of care was (generically) defined in *Blyth* v. *Birmingham Waterworks* (1856) 11 Exch 781.

Blyth v. *Birmingham Waterworks* (1856) 11 Exch 781

Concerning: standard of care

Facts

A wooden plug in a water main became loose in a severe frost. The plug led to a pipe which in turn went up to the street. However, this pipe was blocked with ice, and the water instead flooded the claimant's house. The claimant sued in negligence.

Legal principle

Alderson B defined negligence as:

> The omission to do something which a *reasonable man* guided upon those considerations which ordinarily regulate the conduct of human affairs, would do, or doing something which a *prudent and reasonable man* would not do (emphasis added).

The reasonable person

The conduct of the defendant will be measured against that of the reasonable person. What are the characteristics of such a person? In *Hall* v. *Brooklands Auto-Racing Club* [1933] 1 KB 205, Greer LJ described such a person as:

- 'the man in the street'; or
- 'the man on the Clapham omnibus'; or
- 'the man who takes the magazines at home, and in the evening pushes the lawn mower in his shirt sleeves'.

The reasonable person, therefore, is 'average', not perfect. In deciding whether a defendant has breached the duty of care the court applies an *objective* test. In other words, the general question is 'what would a reasonable person have foreseen in this particular situation?' rather than 'what did this *particular* defendant foresee in this particular situation?'.

Special standards of care

There are certain situations in which the courts apply a different standard of care from that of the reasonable person since the application of the general standard of care as that of the reasonable person would not be suitable:

- Where the defendant has a particular skill
- Where the defendant has a particular *lack* of skill

■ Where the defendant is a child
■ Where the defendant is competing in or watching a sporting event.

Skilled or professional defendants

The standard of care applied to professionals with a particular skill or expertise is that of the reasonable person with the same skill or expertise. For instance, a doctor would be expected to show a greater degree of skill and care to a patient than 'the man on the Clapham omnibus'. This test was established in *Bolam* v. *Friern Hospital Management Committee* [1957] 2 All ER 118.

KEY CASE

Bolam v. *Friern Hospital Management Committee* [1957] 2 All ER 118

Concerning: medical negligence; standard of care

Facts

The claimant underwent a course of electro-convulsive therapy in hospital as treatment for severe depression. This involves the application of electrical current to the patient's head with the aim of causing seizures. The doctor failed to provide the claimant with any muscle relaxants or any physical restraint. The claimant suffered dislocation of both hip joints with fractures of the pelvis on each side. The court had to decide whether it was negligent not to provide relaxants or restraints.

Legal principle

The standard of care for doctors is 'the standard of the ordinary skilled man exercising and professing to have that special skill'. There were conflicting views from practitioners on the use of relaxants and restraints. As there were therefore doctors who *would* have acted in the same way, the doctor treating the claimant had acted in accordance with a competent body of medical opinion and was therefore not negligent.

The decision in *Bolam* has been approved by the House of Lords in subsequent cases (e.g. *Sidaway* v. *Bethlem Royal & Maudsley Hospital Governors* [1985] 1 All ER 643).

The *Bolam* test has also been held to apply to other professionals in general. This has included such diverse professions as:

■ Auctioneers (*Luxmoore-May* v. *Messenger May Baverstock* [1990] 1 WLR 1009)
■ Double glazing window designers (*Adams* v. *Rhymney Valley DC* [2000] Lloyd's Rep PN 777).

However, the *Bolam* test has also been criticised for being too protective of professionals. In medical negligence cases in particular, it has been argued that the test allows practitioners to set their own standards, rather than having those standards set by the courts. The House of Lords clarified the situation in *Bolitho* v. *City and Hackney Health Authority* [1997] 4 All ER 771.

KEY CASE

Bolitho v. *City and Hackney Health Authority* [1997] 4 All ER 771

Concerning: medical negligence; standard of care

Facts

The claimant suffered brain damage as a result of a doctor's failure to attend to clear a child's blocked airways by intubation. There was a difference of medical opinion as to whether intubation was necessary in the particular circumstances.

Legal principle

Although there was a recognised body of medical opinion in accordance with the doctor's practice, the House of Lords held that a doctor *could* be liable in negligence despite the presence of a body of medical opinion in favour of his or her actions. The court can decide that a body of opinion is not reasonable or responsible if it can be demonstrated that the professional opinion is not capable of withstanding logical analysis.

Despite *Bolitho* it remains the case that it is very difficult to prove professional negligence where there is a body of opinion which agrees that the defendant has followed an accepted practice.

Unskilled defendants

The general standard of care in negligence is an objective test, judged against the standards of the reasonable person. This means that no allowance is made for the inexperience or lack of skill of the defendant.

KEY CASE

Nettleship v. *Weston* [1971] 3 All ER 581

Concerning: negligence; unskilled defendants

Facts

A learner driver crashed into a lamp post and injured her instructor.

Legal principle

The driver was liable despite her inexperience. The standard of care required of all motorists is the same: that of the reasonably competent driver.

The same principle has been held to apply in relation to junior doctors such that they are required to reach the standard of the reasonable competent doctor of the same rank (*Wilsher* v. *Essex Area Health Authority* [1986] 3 All ER 801).

Where a person undertakes an activity requiring specialist skills, they are required to reach the standard of a person reasonably competent in that skill (*Wells* v. *Cooper* [1958] 2 QB 265).

Children

Child defendants are expected to reach the standard of care reasonably expected of ordinary children of the same age.

KEY CASE

Mullins v. *Richards* [1998] 1 All ER 920

Concerning: negligence; children

Facts

Two 15-year-old schoolgirls were fencing with plastic rulers during a class when one of the rulers snapped and a fragment of plastic caused one of them to lose all useful sight in one eye.

Legal principle

As Hutchison LJ stated:

> the question for the judge is not whether the actions of the defendant were such as an ordinarily prudent and reasonable adult in the defendant's situation would have realised gave rise to a risk of injury, it is whether an ordinary, prudent and reasonable 15-year-old schoolgirl in the defendant's situation would have realised as such'.

Therefore, since such games were common and rarely led to injury, the injury in question was unforeseeable to 15-year-old schoolgirls, and there was no liability in negligence.

Very young children are, of course, less likely to foresee that their acts might cause harm to others. If so, they will not owe a duty of care and cannot therefore be liable in negligence.

Older children may be judged against the adult standard of care (*Gorely* v. *Codd* [1967] 1 WLR 19). The courts will consider all the circumstances, including the nature of the activity pursued.

Sporting events

Spectators and competitors in sporting events may be owed a *lower* standard of care than the general standard.

KEY CASE

Wooldridge v. *Sumner* [1963] 2 QB 43

Concerning: standard of care owed to spectators

Facts

An experienced rider at an equestrian event galloped his horse around a corner so quickly that the horse went out of control, plunged off the track and injured a photographer in the ensuing chaos.

Legal principle

This was held to be 'an error of judgment' on the part of the rider rather than actionable negligence; furthermore, the Court of Appeal held that the duty of care would only be breached where a competitor demonstrated a 'reckless disregard' for the safety of the spectator.

This test of 'reckless disregard' was extended to fellow competitors in *Harrison* v. *Vincent* [1982] RTR 8. Referees may also owe a duty of care to participants (*Smoldon* v. *Whitworth and Nolan* [1997] PIQR 133).

FURTHER THINKING

For a more detailed discussion of the operation of negligence in relation to sporting events see:

Fafinski, S., 'Consent and the Rules of the Game: the Interplay of Civil and Criminal Liability for Sporting Injuries' (2005) 69.5 *Journal of Criminal Law* 414

Other relevant factors

When determining the standard of care, the courts will take all the circumstances of the case into account. This will possibly involve consideration of a number of other relevant factors including:

- The magnitude of the risk
- The cost and practicability of precautions
- The social value of the defendant's activities
- What the reasonable person would have foreseen.

Many students fail to consider all the circumstances when deciding whether there has been a breach of duty. Therefore, if the facts of the question present an opportunity for you to discuss their possible effects on the standard of care, you should do so.

Magnitude of risk

The magnitude of the risk is determined by the *likelihood* of it occurring and the *seriousness* of the potential injury.

Likelihood of injury

KEY CASES

Bolton v. *Stone* [1951] AC 850; *Miller* v. *Jackson* [1977] QB 966

Concerning: standard of care; likelihood of injury

Facts

Both cases involved damage caused by cricket balls which had been hit out of the ground. In *Bolton* v. *Stone* the ground had been occupied and used as a cricket ground for about 90 years, and there was evidence that on some six occasions in a period of over 30 years a ball had been hit into the highway, but no one had been injured. In *Miller* v. *Jackson* cricket balls were hit out of the ground eight or nine times a season.

Legal principle

A greater risk of damage than normal increases the standard of care required of a potential defendant. Negligence was not found in *Bolton* v. *Stone* but was in *Miller* v. *Jackson*.

Lord Denning provided an entertaining and eloquent counter-argument by way of dissenting judgment in *Miller* v. *Jackson*. It is worth reading to see the difference in view between Lord Denning and the other judges. It demonstrates the amount of discretion judges can have in determining the relevant standard of care 'in all the circumstances'.

reached a higher standard of care where there was an increased likelihood of injury was *Haley* v. *London Electricity Board* [1964] 3 All ER 185. Here a blind claimant fell down a hole dug in the pavement. Given that it is reasonably foreseeable that a blind person could be walking along a pavement, the defendants had a duty to take extra precautions to ensure safety.

Seriousness of injury

If the defendant knows that a specific individual is at risk of suffering greater damage than normal, the defendant may be required to reach a higher standard of care.

KEY CASE

Paris v. *Stepney Borough Council* [1951] AC 367

Concerning: standard of care; seriousness of injury

Facts

The claimant was a mechanic. His employers knew that he was blind in one eye. While the claimant was using a hammer to remove a bolt on a vehicle, a chip of metal flew off and entered his good eye, so injuring it that he became totally blind. The defendants did not provide goggles for him to wear, and there was evidence that it was not the ordinary practice for employers to supply goggles to men employed in garages on the maintenance and repair of vehicles.

Legal principle

The defendants owed a higher standard of care to the claimant because they knew that an injury to his good eye would cause him much more serious consequences than the same injury to a worker with two good eyes.

Cost and practicability of precautions

The court will also take into account what (if any) measures the defendant could have taken to avoid the risk of injury, the cost of those measures and the ease with which they could have been implemented.

KEY CASE

Latimer v. *AEC Ltd* [1953] AC 643

Concerning: standard of care; cost and practicability of precautions

Facts

Owing to an exceptionally heavy storm of rain, a factory was flooded with surface water which became mixed with an oily liquid used as a cooling agent for the machines, which was normally collected in channels in the floor. When the water drained away from the floor, which was level and structurally perfect, it left an oily film on the surface which was slippery. The defendants spread sawdust on the floor, but owing to the unprecedented force of the storm and consequently the large area to be covered, there was insufficient sawdust to cover the whole floor. In the course of his duty the claimant slipped on a portion of the floor not covered with sawdust, fell, and was injured.

> **KEY CASE**
>
> **Legal principle**
>
> The only way to remove the risk would have been to close the affected part of the factory until it had dried out. This would have been expensive and disproportionate to the relatively small risk of injury.

Therefore, the greater the risk of injury, the more a defendant has to do to reduce or eliminate that risk, even if it is costly. The defendant will not generally be able to rely on the fact that the cost of precautions was too expensive to excuse their breach of duty. Impecuniosity is not a defence to a breach of duty.

Social value

Where the defendant's behaviour is in the public interest, it is likely to require the exercise of a *lower* standard of care. In *Daborn* v. *Bath Tramways Motor Co Ltd* [1946] 2 All ER 333, Asquith LJ stated that 'the purpose to be served, if sufficiently important, justifies the assumption of abnormal risk'.

Where human life is at risk, a defendant may also justifiably take abnormal risks (*Watt* v. *Hertfordshire County Council* [1954] 1 WLR 835). However, this does not mean that the defendant is justified in taking *any* risk. Emergency services, for example, must still take care in passing red traffic signals and remember to use their sirens and lights to alert other road users to their presence.

What would the reasonable person have foreseen?

The standard of care is predicated upon what the reasonable person would have foreseen. This depends upon the probability of the consequence. A defendant must take care to avoid 'reasonable probabilities, not fantastic possibilities' (*Fardon* v. *Harcourt-Rivington* [1932] All ER 81).

Proving breach of duty

The legal burden of proving breach of duty is on the claimant. This must be established 'on balance of probabilities'. However, there are certain circumstances in which the claimant may have some assistance. These are:

■ Where the maxim *res ipsa loquitur* applies
■ Where section 11 of the Civil Evidence Act 1968 applies.

Res ipsa loquitur

Res ipsa loquitur is a Latin phrase which means 'the thing speaks for itself'.

In certain circumstances courts will be prepared to find a breach of duty against the defendant without hearing detailed evidence and therefore *prima facie* negligence. There are three conditions which must be satisfied for the claimant to be able to use *res ipsa loquitur*.

KEY CASE

Scott v. *London & St Katherine Docks Co* [1865] 3 H&C 596

Concerning: proof of breach of duty; availability of *res ipsa loquitur*

Facts

The claimant was injured by a sack of sugar which fell from a crane operated by the defendants.

Legal principle

A claimant will be assisted by *res ipsa loquitur* if:

▪ The thing causing the damage is under the control of the defendant or someone for whose negligence the defendant is responsible
▪ The cause of the accident is unknown
▪ The accident is such as would not normally occur without negligence.

Control

The event which causes the damage must be within the control of the defendant. In *Easson* v. *LNER* [1944] 2 KB 421 a four-year-old child fell through the door of a long distance express train while the train was in motion some seven miles from the previous station, and was injured. There was no evidence as to how the door was opened. It was held that the mere fact that the door was opened was not of itself *prima facie* evidence of negligence against the railway company since the railway company could not be expected to be in continuous control of the train doors. A passenger might have been the cause of the accident.

Cause unknown

If the cause of the accident is known, *res ipsa loquitur* cannot apply. The facts do not 'speak for themselves'. Instead, the court must decide on all the facts whether negligence is established (*Barkway* v. *South Wales Transport* [1950] 1 All ER 392).

Accident would not normally occur without negligence

The accident must be such as would not normally occur without negligence. Examples include situations where:

- A large bag of sugar fell from a hoist onto the claimant (*Scott* v. *London and St Katherine Docks Co*)
- A customer slipped on yogurt on a supermarket floor that had not immediately been cleaned up (*Ward* v. *Tesco Stores Ltd* [1976] 1 WLR 810)
- A patient went into hospital with two stiff fingers and came out with four stiff fingers (*Cassidy* v. *Ministry of Health* [1951] 2 KB 343).

The effect of *res ipsa loquitur*

If *res ipsa loquitur* is available then it raises a *prima facie* presumption of negligence against the defendant. The defendant must then explain how the accident could have occurred without negligence. If the defendant succeeds, then the claimant must try to prove the defendant's negligence. This will be difficult, since, if negligence could be proved it is unlikely that the claimant would have relied on *res ipsa loquitur* in the first place. The burden of proof does not shift from the claimant (*Ng Chun Pui* v. *Lee Cheun Tat* [1988] RTR 298).

EXAM TIP

It is a common mistake to state that *res ipsa loquitur reverses* the legal burden of proof, such that the defendant must show that the damage was not caused by failure to reach the required standard of care. This is not so. The burden remains on the claimant throughout. This was made clear by the decision of the Privy Council in *Ng Chun Pui*.

Civil Evidence Act 1968

Claimants in negligence proceedings may also be assisted by section 11 of the Civil Evidence Act 1968.

KEY STATUTORY PROVISION

Civil Evidence Act 1968, section 11

11 Convictions as evidence in civil proceedings

. . .

(2) In any civil proceedings in which by virtue of this section a person is proved to have been convicted of an offence by or before any court in the United Kingdom or by a court-martial there or elsewhere—

(a) he shall be taken to have committed that offence unless the contrary is proved . . .

Therefore, if the defendant has been convicted of a criminal offence by a UK court, this is taken as proof that the defendant *did* commit it in any associated civil proceedings unless the contrary is proved. If the defendant has been convicted of an offence which includes negligent conduct, then the burden of proof shifts to the defendant to prove that there was no negligence. Examples of such offences include:

■ Careless, and inconsiderate, driving (section 3 Road Traffic Act 1998, as substituted)
■ Gross negligence manslaughter.

Chapter summary:
Putting it all together

TEST YOURSELF

☐ Can you tick all the points from the revision checklist at the beginning of this chapter?

☐ Take the **end-of-chapter quiz** on the companion website.

☐ Test your knowledge of the cases with the **revision flashcards** on the website.

☐ Attempt the problem question from the beginning of the chapter using the guidelines below.

☐ Go to the companion website to try out other questions.

Answer guidelines

See the problem question at the start of the chapter. A diagram illustrating how to structure your answer is available on the website.

This discussion will only consider duty of care and breach of duty. Causation and remoteness will be covered in the next chapter.

1 Problem questions involving negligence often concern multiple claims. One useful technique in untangling the potential claims is to work your way through the question looking for parties that have suffered loss or damage. Remember that there can be no negligence claim without loss or damage. Once you have identified the possible claimants, then look for all potential defendants and consider the four requirements of negligence.

   ■ **Roy** appears to have suffered no loss or damage. There is nothing to suggest that his trailer was damaged, and even if it was it would have been as a result of his own carelessness.

- **Wayne** suffered the loss of his scooter and ultimately his life.
- **Chelsea** suffered no loss or injury.
- **Dave**, the instructor, sustained a severe whiplash injury and £4000 damage to his car.
- **Flo** lost her crop of potentially prize-winning marrows.
- Roy owed Wayne, Chelsea and Dave a duty of care as between road users. This is an established duty situation and an application of the general neighbour principle from *Donoghue* v. *Stevenson* as reformulated in *Caparo* v. *Dickman*.
- Similarly Wayne and Chelsea owed a general duty of care to other road users. Chelsea, in particular, owed a duty of care to Dave, her instructor. Dave also owes Chelsea a duty of care as her instructor.
- Does Roy owe Flo a duty of care? Would she have been in his contemplation as potentially being affected by Roy's failure to hitch the trailer up properly – or would this have been a 'fantastic possibility'?
- Roy was in breach of his duty of care to the other road users. He fell below the standard of the reasonable driver with trailer by failing to ensure that the trailer was properly covered (*Blyth* v. *Birmingham Waterworks*). Moreover, he was convicted of careless driving. Section 11 of the Civil Evidence Act 1968 will apply. This will assist claimants against Roy.
- Chelsea's inexperience will be irrelevant (*Nettleship* v. *Weston*).
- Dr Roberts owed Wayne a duty of care. The doctor–patient relationship is another established duty situation.
- Was Dr Roberts in breach of duty? Although he was only a junior doctor on his second day, *Bolam* v. *Friern Hospital Management Committee* requires him to reach the standard of the ordinary skilled doctor of his level. However, did he act in accordance with a recognised body of medical opinion? There was a school of thought that some doctors might also have sent Wayne home. If so, *Bolam* would suggest that Dr Roberts was not in breach. However, if *Bolitho* is followed despite there being a recognised body of medical opinion in accordance with Dr Roberts' practice, a doctor *can* be liable in negligence if it can be demonstrated that the professional opinion is not capable of withstanding logical analysis.

Make your answer really stand out:

- Do not waste words on claims which cannot succeed. If you cannot establish a duty of care in relation to the defendant and claimant, there is no point in going on to discuss the other elements of negligence because there is no claim. Do not assume that all parties mentioned in the question will have a claim; one way in which to demonstrate your understanding of negligence would be to point out when a party has no claim and to explain why this is so.
- Remember to include clear and concise explanations of key concepts. This question includes a specialist level of skill (doctor) as well as an experienced

defendant (learner driver). As well as covering the liability of the parties, it would enhance your answer to provide a brief explanation of why there is a departure from the general standard of care in these situations, drawing reference to the policy of the courts.

■ Remember to present both sides of the argument (for and against liability) as much as possible, making use of the relevant facts to support your argument. Do not let your answer turn into an abstract discussion of the law as this will result in lost marks. Make sure that every paragraph makes some mention of facts taken from the question.

2
Negligence – causation and remoteness of damage

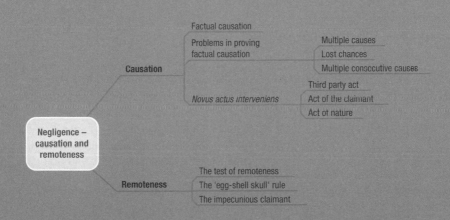

- **Causation**
  - Factual causation
  - Problems in proving factual causation
    - Multiple causes
    - Lost chances
    - Multiple consecutive causes
  - *Novus actus interveniens*
    - Third party act
    - Act of the claimant
    - Act of nature
- **Negligence – causation and remoteness**
- **Remoteness**
  - The test of remoteness
  - The 'egg-shell skull' rule
  - The impecunious claimant

Revision checklist

What you need to know:

- [ ] Explain factual causation and apply the 'but for' test.
- [ ] Identify and address the problems posed by multiple causes
- [ ] Appreciate the difficulties of establishing a 'lost chance'
- [ ] The meaning of *novus actus interveniens* and its impact on causation
- [ ] The principles and policies involved in remoteness of damage.

Introduction
Causation and remoteness

Causation and remoteness provide the link between the defendant's negligent conduct and the harm suffered by the claimant.

The previous chapter covered duty of care and breach of duty whilst this chapter focuses on causation and remoteness. Students tend to find duty and standard of care relatively straightforward but often struggle with principles of causation and remoteness. This means that these topics are frequently ignored by students and left out of both revision and exam answers, which leads to an inevitable loss of marks. It may help to focus on causation and remoteness in very simple terms and gradually build upon your understanding as you work through the chapter. Causation requires that there is a link between the defendant's negligence and the claimant's injury (did the defendant cause the harm?) whilst remoteness eliminates causes that are too distant from the original negligence to be recoverable (is there a strong enough link between the negligence and the damage?)

Essay question advice

As causation and remoteness are not popular topics, students tend to avoid questions involving these issues. It is often the case that when essays on these topics appear in examinations as the only essays on negligence, students who have revised duty and breach tackle the questions on the basis of this revision and skirt over, or ignore altogether, issues of causation and remoteness. This is an extremely poor strategy; you *must* answer the question that appears on the exam paper, not the question that you hoped would appear. To adapt the question to the material that you have revised does not attract any credit; you would be better placed answering an entirely different question. However, the problem can be avoided with careful revision of causation and remoteness.

Problem question advice

Again, students frequently ignore issues of causation and remoteness in problem questions. To do so deprives you of a whole section of marks. Any answer to a problem question on negligence must cover all four elements on the tort so it is essential that you are able to demonstrate an understanding of causation and remoteness in addition to duty and breach. It is worth the effort to get to grip with these topics; negligence is a favourite topic with examiners and the ability to address aspects of the tort that are neglected by other students will set your answer apart from the others'.

Sample question

You can find the question for this chapter on page 3. The duty and breach elements were covered in Chapter 1. Guidelines on addressing the causation and remoteness parts of the question are included at the end of the chapter, whilst a sample essay question and guidance on tackling it can be found on the companion website.

Problem question

Refer back to Chapter 1, page 3 for the problem question.

■ Causation

The claimant must show a causal link between the defendant's act or omission and the loss or damage suffered. This is often referred to as the 'chain of causation'.

Factual causation

The breach of duty must be the factual cause of the damage. The general test used by the courts to determine factual causation is known as the 'but for' test.

KEY CASE

***Cork* v. *Kirby MacLean Ltd* [1952] 2 All ER 402**

Concerning: causation; 'but for' test

Facts

A workman, an epileptic, was set to work painting the roof inside a factory, which necessitated his doing the work from a platform some 23 feet above the floor of the factory. The platform was some 27 inches wide and was used

▶

for the deposit of the workman's bucket and brush. There were no guard-rails or toe-boards. The workman fell from the platform and was killed.

Legal principle

Lord Denning stated that:

> ... if the damage would not have happened *but for* [emphasis added] a particular fault, then that fault is the cause of the damage; if it would have happened just the same, fault or no fault, the fault is not the cause of the damage.

The question to be asked as a starting point in establishing factual causation is 'but for the defendant's breach of duty, would the loss or damage have occurred?'. The facts of the case often mean that the application of the test is straightforward:

Barnett v. *Chelsea and Kensington Hospital Management Committee* [1969] 1 QB 428

Concerning: causation; 'but for' test

Facts

A patient was turned away from a casualty department by a doctor who refused to examine him. He later died of arsenic poisoning. It was shown that the man would not have recovered even if the doctor had treated him.

Legal principle

The hospital was not liable for the clear breach of duty in failing to treat the patient. The failure to treat was not the cause of death. The patient would have died just the same.

Problems in proving factual causation

Although the 'but for' test might seem straightforward, there are situations in which proving factual causation is more difficult. This can occur in cases involving:

- Multiple causes of damage
- A 'lost chance' of recovery
- Multiple *consecutive* causes of damage.

Multiple causes of damage

Where there is more than one possible cause of harm to the claimant, the claimant does not have to show that the defendant's breach of duty was the *only* cause of damage or even the *main* cause of damage.

KEY CASE

Bonnington Castings Ltd v. *Wardlaw* [1956] AC 613

Concerning: causation; multiple causes of damage

Facts

The claimant contracted pneumoconiosis after working for years in dusty conditions. There were two main causes of dust in the foundry, one of which was required by law to be extracted. It was impossible to prove which dust the claimant had inhaled.

Legal principle

Since the dust which should have been extracted was at least a partial cause of the damage, the defendant was liable in negligence. The claimant therefore only needs to show that a defendant's breach of duty '*materially contributed*' to the damage.

This was relatively straightforward, since there were only two possible causes of damage. However, particularly in medical negligence cases, there may be too many possible causes for the claimant to discharge the burden of proof on balance of probabilities.

KEY CASE

Wilsher v. *Essex Area Health Authority* [1988] 1 All ER 871

Concerning: causation; multiple causes of damage; balance of probabilities

Facts

The claimant was born prematurely and needed extra oxygen to survive. A junior doctor inserted a catheter into a vein rather than an artery. As a result the baby received too much oxygen, which caused damage to the retina and consequent blindness.

There were five possible causes of the baby's blindness. It was impossible to say which of the five competing and different scenarios had actually happened.

Legal principle

Causation was not established. Since none of the potential causes was more likely to have happened than any of the others the balance of probabilities was not satisfied.

Therefore, taking *Bonnington Castings* and *Wilsher* together, where there is more than one cause, the defendant's breach must be the *substantial cause* of the damage.

The defendant may also be liable if the breach of duty materially increases the risk of damage.

KEY CASE

McGhee v. *National Coal Board* [1973] 3 All ER 1008

Concerning: causation; multiple causes of damage; material increase of risk

Facts

The claimant was employed to clean out brick kilns. The working conditions were hot, dirty and dusty, but the defendants provided no adequate washing facilities. After some days working in the brick kilns the claimant was found to be suffering from dermatitis. The evidence also showed that the fact that after work the claimant had had to exert himself further by bicycling home with brick dust adhering to his skin had added materially to the risk that he might develop the disease.

Legal principle

Although the employer was not liable for injury resulting from the claimant's exposure to dust in the normal course of his work, it had materially increased his risk of doing so, since the failure to provide washing facilities meant the claimant was caked in dust for longer then required as he cycled home. The employer was found liable in negligence for materially increasing the risk.

The *McGhee* test was used in favour of the claimant by the House of Lords in *Fairchild* v. *Glenhaven Funeral Servies Ltd* [2003] 3 WLR 89.

'Lost chance' cases

The courts are extremely reluctant to impose liability where the negligence of the defendant caused the claimant to lose a chance.

KEY CASE

Hotson v. *East Berkshire Area Health Authority* [1987] 2 All ER 909

Concerning: causation; lost chance

Facts

A boy fractured his hip when he fell from a tree. The hospital made a misdiagnosis and the boy developed a hip deformity. Experts confirmed that he would have had a 75% chance of developing the deformity with a correct

▶

KEY CASE

diagnosis. The Court of Appeal upheld the decision of the trial judge who awarded the boy 25% of the damages that were considered appropriate for his injury for his lost chance of recovery. The Health Authority appealed to the House of Lords.

Legal principle

The decision of the Court of Appeal was reversed. The House of Lords considered that, since there was only a 25% chance that the negligence had caused the boy's injuries, this did not satisfy the balance of probabilities.

Multiple consecutive causes of damage

Where there are consecutive causes of damage, the application of the 'but for' test is applied to the *original defendant*.

KEY CASE

Performance Cars Ltd v. *Abraham* [1962] 1 QB 33

Concerning: multiple consecutive causes

Facts

The first defendant negligently drove into a Rolls Royce. The Rolls Royce was later negligently struck by another car, driven by the second defendant.

Legal principle

The first defendant remained liable. The second defendant was not liable for the cost of the respray since the car already needed a respray at the time of the collision with the second defendant.

Novus actus interveniens

KEY DEFINITION

Novus actus interveniens is a Latin phrase which means 'a new act intervenes'.

An intervening act may break the chain of causation between the defendant's breach of duty and the loss or damage suffered by the claimant (see Figure 2.1). If the *novus actus interveniens* is sufficient to break the chain, then the defendant may not be liable despite being in breach of the duty of care. The intervening act may be:

▪ A third party act;
▪ An act of the claimant; or
▪ An act of nature.

Figure 2.1

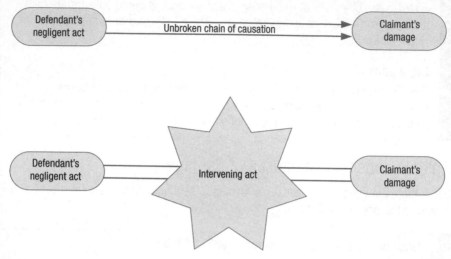

Third party act

For a third party act:

■ The original defendant will be liable where the intervening act does not cause the loss. The original defendant will be responsible for 'injury and damage which are the natural and probable results of the [initial] wrongful act (*Knightley* v. *Johns* [1982] 1 All ER 851)

■ The original defendant will be liable where the intervening act is one that should have been foreseen (*Lamb* v. *Camden London Borough Council* [1981] QB 625).

The question of whether an intervening event will break the chain of causation is one for the courts to decide in all the circumstances.

KEY CASES

Baker v. *Willoughby* [1969] 3 All ER 1528; *Jobling* v. *Associated Dairies Ltd* [1982] 2 All ER 752

Concerning: *novus actus interveniens*; third party acts

Facts

In *Baker* v. *Willoughby* the claimant was knocked down by a car due to the negligent driving of the defendant. He suffered a permanent stiff leg as a result. After the accident, but before the trial, he was shot in the injured leg during a robbery at work. As a result his leg was amputated.

In *Jobling* v. *Associated Dairies* the claimant was injured at work due to his employer's negligence. He slipped and injured his back and lost 50% of his

KEY CASE earning capacity as a result. Three years later, he developed spondylotic myelopathy, a spinal disease. This had not been brought about by the accident. He was consequently unable to work.

Legal principle

In *Baker* the court held that the gunman's act was not a *novus actus interveniens* and the defendant remained liable. The claimant's loss of earnings was a result of the original injury. The later robbery and consequent amputation did not change this, even though the eventual damage was different and more severe.

In *Jobling* the disease of the spine *was* held to be a *novus actus interveniens* which did break the chain of causation.

Act of the claimant

In this case, the *novus actus interveniens* will mean that the claimant is responsible for his own damage.

KEY CASE

McKew v. Holland & Hannen & Cubitts (Scotland) Ltd [1969] 3 All ER 1621

Concerning: *novus actus interveniens*; act of the claimant

Facts

As a result of the defendants' negligence, the claimant suffered a leg injury. This left his leg seriously weakened. He later fell when attempting to descend a steep flight of steps with no handrail, suffering further serious injuries. He did not seek assistance in climbing the stairs.

Legal principle

The claimant's act in attempting to descend a steep staircase without a handrail in the normal manner and without adult assistance when his leg had previously given way on occasions was unreasonable. The court held that his act was a *novus actus interveniens* which had broken the chain of causation. As a result the defendants were not liable in damages for his second injury.

In order for the act of a claimant to be a *novus actus interveniens*, it must be entirely unreasonable in all the circumstances.

REVISION NOTE

If the claimant partially contributes to their own damage or injury, this may raise issues of contributory negligence which is covered in Chapter 11. This will generally lead to a reduction in their damages.

Act of nature

Intervening acts of nature will not generally break the chain of causation. However, the defendant will not normally be liable where the intervening act of nature is unforeseeable and separate from the initial negligent act or omission.

> **KEY CASE**
>
> ### *Carslogie Steamship Co Ltd* v. *Royal Norwegian Government* [1952] AC 292
>
> **Concerning:** *novus actus interveniens*; act of nature
>
> **Facts**
>
> The claimant's ship was damaged following a collision. After temporary repairs, the ship then set off on a voyage to a port in the United States where permanent repairs could be carried out. During her voyage across the Atlantic the ship sustained further heavy weather damage during a storm.
>
> **Legal principle**
>
> The defendants were not liable for the damage caused by the storm. The court held that the storm could have happened on any voyage and therefore the storm damage was not a consequence of the collision. It was unforeseeable and quite separate.

■ Remoteness

The final element required in establishing negligence is the extent of the damage suffered by the claimant which should be attributable to the defendant. In other words, for how much of the claimant's loss should the defendant be responsible?

> **REVISION NOTE**
>
> Remoteness is sometimes referred to as 'legal causation' or 'causation in law'.

The test of remoteness

> **KEY CASE**
>
> ### *Re Polemis and Furness, Withy & Co Ltd* [1921] 3 KB 560
>
> **Concerning: remoteness of damage**
>
> **Facts**
>
> The charterers of a ship filled the hold with a cargo including a number of containers of petrol. These filled the hold with petrol vapour which ignited when a heavy plank was dropped into the hold by a stevedore whilst the ship was unloading, destroying the ship.

►

> **KEY CASE**
>
> **Legal principle**
>
> The defendants were liable for *all* damage which resulted from the breach of duty, regardless of whether that damage was foreseeable by the defendant. As Scrutton LJ stated:
>
> > ... if the act would or might probably cause damage, the fact that the damage it in fact causes is not the exact kind of damage one would expect is immaterial, so long as the damage is in fact directly traceable to the negligent act.

The test in *Re Polemis* does not limit liability for the direct consequences of a negligent act, however severe or unforeseeable those consequences may be. It has been criticised for its unfairness in that respect. Similar circumstances arose in *Overseas Tankship (UK) Ltd* v. *Morts Dock and Engineering Co Ltd (The Wagon Mound) (No 1)* [1961] 1 All ER 404.

> **KEY CASE**
>
> ***Overseas Tankship (UK) Ltd* v. *Morts Dock and Engineering Co Ltd (The Wagon Mound) (No 1)* [1961] 1 All ER 404**
>
> **Concerning: remoteness of damage**
>
> **Facts**
>
> The defendants negligently leaked a quantity of bunkering oil into Sydney Harbour from a tanker. This oil drifted into the claimant's wharf where it mixed with assorted detritus including cotton wadding. Welding was taking place in the wharf. The claimants sought (and received) assurances that it was safe for them to continue welding. However, sparks from the welding ignited the oily wadding which caused fire to spread to two ships, damaging them. The wharf was also fouled.
>
> **Legal principle**
>
> At first instance, the trial judge applied the principles from *Re Polemis*, finding that the defendants were liable for the fire damage, since the fouling to the wharf was a foreseeable consequence of the leakage. On appeal, the Privy Council reversed the decision, holding that the correct test for remoteness is reasonable foreseeability of the kind or type of damage in fact suffered by the claimant.

The tests in *Re Polemis* and *The Wagon Mound (No 1)* cannot be reconciled. The decision in *Re Polemis* was taken by the Court of Appeal and has never been overruled, since *The Wagon Mound (No 1)* was heard by the Privy Council. As such, both cases remain good law. However, *The Wagon Mound (No 1)* is now accepted by the courts (including the Court of Appeal) as the relevant test to follow in questions of remoteness.

The 'egg-shell skull' rule

If the type of injury is foreseeable, but the severity of the injury is not, due to some pre-existing special condition on the part of the claimant, then the defendant remains liable for *all* the losses.

KEY CASE

Smith v. *Leech Brain & Co Ltd* [1961] 3 All ER 1159

Concerning: remoteness; the 'egg-shell skull' rule

Facts

The claimant was splashed by molten metal as a result of his employer's negligence and suffered a burn to his lip. This burn triggered cancer, from which the claimant died. The claimant's lip was pre-malignant at the time of the incident.

Legal principle

Some form of harm from the burn was foreseeable although the particular type of harm in the particular circumstances was not. However, despite the fact that death from cancer was not a foreseeable consequence of the burn, the employers remained liable in negligence for the full extent of the damage.

In essence, the 'egg-shell skull' rule means that defendants must take their victims as they find them.

REVISION NOTE

The 'egg-shell skull' rule also applies in cases of psychiatric harm. See Chapter 3.

The impecunious claimant

One particular situation where the 'egg-shell skull' rule has been held *not* to apply is in cases where the losses result from the claimant's lack of means.

KEY CASE

Liesbosch Dredger v. *SS Edison* [1933] AC 449

Concerning: remoteness; the 'egg-shell skull' rule

Facts

The claimant's dredger sank due to the defendant's negligence. They could not afford to replace the lost dredger. In order to fulfil their contractual obligations, the claimants hired a dredger at an exorbitant rate.

Legal principle

The claimants could not recover the high rental charges since these were a result of their own lack of means and not 'immediate physical consequences' of the negligent act.

The *Liesbosch* has been distinguished by the Court of Appeal in cases relating to mitigation of loss (*Perry* v. *Sidney Phillips* [1982] 3 All ER 705) and subsequently only considered to apply in 'exceptional circumstances' (Mattocks v. *Mann* [1993] RTR 13).

Chapter summary:
Putting it all together

TEST YOURSELF

☐ Can you tick all the points from the revision checklist at the beginning of this chapter?

☐ Take the **end-of-chapter quiz** on the companion website.

☐ Test your knowledge of the cases with the **revision flashcards** on the website.

☐ Attempt the remainder of the problem question from the beginning of Chapter 1 using the guidelines below.

☐ Go to the companion website to try out other questions.

Answer guidelines

See the problem question at the start of Chapter 1. A diagram illustrating how to structure your answer is available on the website.

1 Although there is a separation of duty and breach on the one hand and causation

and remoteness on the other in this book, this reflects the structure and length of the chapters. In dealing with a problem question on negligence, it would be important not to adopt this approach but to deal with each party individually and to address all four points (duty, breach, causation, remoteness).

2 When addressing these four issues, remember to stop if it is clear that one of the elements is not satisfied; there is no point discussing remoteness if you have not been able to establish causation. For example, Chelsea owes a duty of care to other road users, including her driving instructor, Dave. She has breached that duty by confusing the brake and accelerator pedals and this falls below the standard of driving expected of the reasonably competent driver. It is irrelevant that she is taking her first lesson or is in the presence of her instructor as she is judged on the standard of the ordinary driver, not the inexperienced driver (*Nettleship* v. *Weston*). Causation can be established as 'but for' her breach of duty, Dave would not have suffered whiplash or £4000's worth of damage to his car. The injury and damage were foreseeable consequences of Chelsea's careless driving, thus not too remote (*Wagon Mound (No 1)*). Chelsea is therefore liable to Dave in negligence.

Make your answer really stand out

■ When dealing with complex issues, make sure that you demonstrate your understanding with clear and simple explanations. As part of your revision process, make sure you can write a few sentences that explain key concepts such as causation and remoteness. Once you can do this and use some of the key cases outlined in this chapter to add weight to your answer, you will have a good basis upon which to apply the law.

■ Make sure you deal with causation and remoteness thoroughly (remoteness in particular is often left out altogether by students). Demonstrating an ability to deal with issues known to be difficult will really impress your examiner.

3
Special duties

```
                          Damage to property
        Economic loss     Acquisition of defective
                          goods/property


        Negligent misstatement    Hedley Byrne v. Heller
                                  Liability to third parties


                          Definition of psychiatric injury
                                                    Primary victims
                                          Duty of care
                                                    Secondary victims
Special duties   Psychiatric injury
                                          Proximity
                          Elements of the tort  How the shock was caused
                                          Remoteness  The 'egg-shell skull' rule
```

Revision checklist

What you need to know:

☐ The definition of economic loss and the limited circumstances under which it may be recoverable

☐ The changes to the extent of economic loss introduced by *Anns*, *Junior Books* and *Murphy*.

☐ The principles of negligent misstatement

☐ The definition of psychiatric injury and how it applies to primary and secondary victims.

Introduction:
Special duties

There are certain categories of claim in negligence that require separate consideration as the core legal principles have been adapted to their particular circumstances.

This chapter covers three of those situations: pure economic loss, negligent misstatement and psychiatric injury. There has been a large volume of case law that examines these issues and it can seem rather complicated, particularly in relation to economic loss, so the topics do require careful consideration. They are important areas of revision since examiners often like to test the more detailed knowledge that they require. What's more, what might seem like a fairly standard question on negligence might involve one of the parties suffering psychiatric harm or economic loss. Without a good understanding of these special situations you would be unable to do well on the whole question and your marks would suffer as a result.

Essay question advice

Essay questions on special duties could concentrate on one of them in particular or cover all of them in a much broader-ranging evaluation of the role of the duty of care in negligence. Such questions would tend to be unpopular with students as the special duty situations are often overlooked in selective revision. This means that equipped with a good understanding of the special duty situations you would be well placed for your answer to stand out among those of your more ill-prepared colleagues. Remember that unpopular questions tend to be done either very well, or very badly.

Special duty situations can be mixed in with standard duty situations very easily. In a negligence scenario. For example, in a negligence scenario involving three parties, one might suffer physical loss or damage, one might suffer economic loss and another psychiatric harm. If you had just focused your revision on 'standard' negligence, you could lose out on up to 40% of the marks available for such a question, as you could not comment well on the special duty situations. This could make the difference between a first and a fail! As with negligence, remember to be methodical when applying the law relating to the special duty situations to the facts given and work through each of the elements of the duty in turn.

Sample question

Could you answer this question? Below is a typical problem question that could arise on this topic. Guidelines on answering the question are included at the end of the chapter, whilst a sample essay question and guidance on tackling it can be found on the companion website.

Problem question

Brenda dropped her grandson, Eddie, off at the bus station so that he could catch his bus home after he had come to visit for the weekend. She then went to her church meeting. Unfortunately, Eddie's bus had to swerve to avoid a lorry driven by Sid, who had fallen asleep at the wheel. The bus crashed into a petrol tanker and caught fire.

Brenda heard the next morning that Eddie had been on the bus and had died in the fire. She suffered a complete nervous breakdown.

Simon, who was off work with a stress-related problem, heard the crash and ran to the scene where he spent two hours pulling severely burnt passengers from the burning wreckage of the bus. As a result Simon is now suffering from post-traumatic stress disorder.

Does Brenda or Simon have a viable claim in negligence?

■ Economic loss

KEY DEFINITION

Economic loss refers to financial losses which are not attributable to physical harm caused to the claimant or his property. It includes loss of profits, loss of trade and loss of investment revenue.

There is a separate set of rules relating to economic loss because the courts have felt the need to ensure that a defendant does not attract limitless liability as a result of his actions. Most conduct that amounts to a tort affects a finite number of people and gives rise to largely determinate harm. The sorts of situations that fall within pure economic loss tend to lack these limiting factors so a defendant could be liable to a large number of claimants on the basis of a single incident. For example, if a lorry crashes into an electricity substation as a result of negligent driving and the electricity supply to an industrial estate and shopping centre is cut off for eight hours, the extent of the financial losses would be immense. Such potentially limitless liability would make it impossible to obtain insurance to cover such losses thus creating an even more difficult situation if all economic loss was actionable.

Pure economic loss which is not consequential on physical damage to the claimant's property is *not recoverable* in tort. Therefore, most cases turn on whether or not the particular loss suffered is pure economic loss. Economic losses can be caused by:

▌ Damage to property
▌ Acquisition of defective goods or property.

Damage to property

Economic loss which is a direct consequence of physical damage is an exception to the general rule that economic loss is not recoverable in tort.

> **KEY CASE**
>
> *Spartan Steel and Alloys Ltd* v. *Martin & Co (Contractors) Ltd* [1973] 1 QB 27
>
> **Concerning: consequential economic loss**
>
> **Facts**
>
> The claimants manufactured stainless steel alloys at a factory 24 hours a day. The defendants' employees, who were working on a nearby road, damaged the electrical supply cable to the factory. The electricity board shut off the power supply to the factory for 14½ hours until the cable was mended. The claimants scrapped a 'melt' in the furnace, reducing its value by £368. If the supply had not been cut off, they would have made a profit of £400 on the melt, and £1767 on another four melts, which would have been put into the furnace. They claimed damages from the defendants in respect of all three sums.
>
> **Legal principle**
>
> The claimants could recover the damage to the melt in progress and the loss of profit on that melt. They could not recover for the loss of profit during the time that the electricity was switched off. The damage to the melt in progress was physical damage and the loss of profit on it was a direct consequence of the physical damage. The further loss of profit was pure economic loss and not recoverable.

In *Spartan Steel and Alloys* Lord Denning said:

> I think the question of recovering economic loss is one of policy. Whenever the courts draw a line to mark out the bounds of duty they do it as to limit the responsibility of the defendant ... It seems to me better to consider the particular relationship in hand and see whether or not, as a matter of policy, economic loss should be recoverable or not.

Acquisition of defective goods or property

The general position in relation to the claimant acquiring defective goods or property is the same as for other cases of economic loss: the loss is not recoverable in tort.

However, there has been a series of cases in which this position was relaxed.

KEY CASE

Anns v. *Merton London Borough Council* [1978] AC 728

Concerning: economic loss

Facts

The claimants were tenants of a block of flats built in accordance with plans approved by the council. The foundations were too shallow. The tenants sued for the cost of making the flats safe on the basis that the council either negligently approved inadequate plans or failed to inspect the foundations during construction.

Legal principle

A duty of care was owed by the council and that if their inspectors did not exercise proper care and skill then the council was liable even though the loss suffered was economic loss.

KEY CASE

Junior Books Ltd v. *Veitchi Co Ltd* [1983] 1 AC 520

Concerning: economic loss

Facts

The claimants were having a factory built. On the advice of their architect, they subcontracted the defendants to complete the work. The defendants laid an unusable floor which had to be replaced. The claimants sued for the costs of replacing the floor and the loss of profit while the floor was relaid.

Legal principle

Even though the claimants had suffered no physical damage, they

KEY CASE

successfully recovered all the heads of loss claimed, despite their all being economic loss. The court considered that, in all the circumstances, the proximity of the parties was only 'just short of a direct contractual relationship'.

These decisions appeared to mark a significant departure from the general principle that economic loss was not recoverable in tort. The courts almost immediately tried to limit the effects of *Anns* and *Junior Books*. Although *Junior Books* has not yet been overruled, it has never been followed – the courts have always distinguished it on its particular facts. There are a number of examples where courts rejected claims for pure economic loss based on *Anns* (for example, *D & F Estates Ltd* v. *Church Commissioners for England* [1989] AC 177).

The House of Lords finally clarified the situation in *Murphy* v. *Brentwood District Council* [1990] 2 All ER 908.

KEY CASE

Murphy v. *Brentwood District Council* [1990] 2 All ER 908

Concerning: economic loss

Facts

A council approved plans for a concrete raft upon which properties were built. The raft moved and caused cracks in the walls of a property which was sold for £35,000 less that it would have done had it not been defective.

Legal principle

The House of Lords overruled *Anns* and held that the council was not liable in the absence of physical injury.

In summary, then, *economic loss arising from a negligent act or omission is not recoverable*.

Negligent misstatement

Liability in tort is based upon the defendant's conduct or, occasionally, his failure to act. It was long accepted that negligent or unintentional statements, however inaccurate or misleading, could not provide the basis for an action to recover financial loss caused by reliance on that statement. For example, in *Candler* v. *Crane Christmas & Co* [1951] 2 KB 533, investors were not able to recover money lost as a consequence of their reliance on negligently prepared accounts.

Hedley Byrne v. Heller

It was not until the landmark case of *Hedley Byrne* v. *Heller* that the House of Lords established that liability in tort could be founded upon a negligent misstatement:

KEY CASE

Hedley Byrne v. *Heller and Partners Ltd* [1964] AC 465

Concerning: liability for negligent misstatement

Facts

The claimant was an advertising company that was offered work by a small company with whom they had no previous dealings. It sought a reference from the company's bank which was prepared without any checks being made into the current state of its finances. In reliance upon the bank's reference, the claimant carried out work for the company which then went into liquidation before any payment was made. The claimant sought to recover its losses from the defendant bank on the basis of its negligent misstatement.

Legal principle

The House of Lords held that there were circumstances in which a person could be liable in tort for losses caused by a statement which he made if he did not take sufficient care to ensure that his statement was accurate or if he did not make it clear that he had taken no steps to ensure its accuracy.

As this opened a new area of tortious liability, the House of Lords imposed strict limitations upon the situations which would give rise to liability. A special relationship must exist between the parties before there is a possibility of liability for negligent misstatement that causes economic loss; see Figure 3.1.

Figure 3.1

(1) The relationship will exist if one party exercises skill and judgement and the other party acts in reliance of this skill and judgement

(2) The person making the statement must possess skill in relation to the particular statement that is made and should realise that the other party will act in reliance upon the statement

(3) The party to whom the statement is made must have acted in reliance with that statement in circumstances where it was reasonable for him to rely upon the statement

Examples of the 'special relationship' under *Hedley Byrne* v. *Heller* include that between:

- An environmental health inspector and the owners of a guest house (*Walton* v. *North Cornwall District Council* [1997] 1 WLR 570)
- A bank clerk advising on a mortgage (*Cornish* v. *Midland Bank plc* [1985] 3 All ER 513)
- A friend (holding himself out as having some knowledge about cars) purchasing a car on his friend's behalf (*Chaudry* v. *Prabhakar* [1989] 1 WLR 29).

The criteria from *Hedley Byrne* v. *Heller* were restated in *Caparo Industries plc* v. *Dickman*.

REVISION NOTE

Caparo Industries v. *Dickman* was also covered in Chapter 1 on the duty of care in negligence as it provides a general restatement of the duty of care from *Donoghue* v. *Stevenson*.

KEY CASE

Caparo Industries plc v. Dickman [1990] 1 All ER 568

Concerning: negligent misstatement; proximity

Facts

Set out in Chapter 1.

Legal principle

To establish a claim in negligent misstatement, in particular to proximity of relationship, the claimant must prove that the defendant must have known:

- The statement would be communicated to the claimant
- The statement would be made specifically in connection with a particular transaction
- The claimant would be very likely to rely upon it in deciding whether or not to proceed with the transaction.

Liability to third parties

Where the defendant makes a statement which is communicated to the claimant by a third party and the claimant suffers loss, there still may be sufficient proximity for liability to arise for the defendant's negligent misstatement as long as there is a special relationship between defendant and claimant (*Spring* v. *Guardian Assurance plc* [1994] 2 WLR 354; *White* v. *Jones* [1995] 1 All ER 691).

■ Psychiatric injury

At first glance, liability for psychiatric injury seems to have little in common with liability for economic loss. However, both issues raise the prospect of potentially limitless claims as a single event could affect a multitude of people. Just as an interruption in electricity supply could affect hundreds of businesses in the surrounding area, a single traumatic event could be witnessed by many people, some of whom may be particularly susceptible to psychiatric injury. In addition to concerns about 'opening the floodgates' to limitless claims, there are also problems in establishing that any particular individual has suffered a psychiatric injury that is attributable to the defendant's negligence.

Definition of psychiatric injury

One means of limiting the potential number of claimants is the stipulation that the psychiatric injury suffered must be a *medically recognised condition*. A number of different conditions have been tested by case law, as the table below shows.

Medically recognised	Not medically recognised
Post-traumatic stress disorder (*Leach* v. *Chief Constable of Gloucestershire Constabulary* [1999] 1 All ER 215)	Distress (*Kralj* v. *McGrath* [1986] 1 All ER 54)
Pathological grief (*Vernon* v. *Bosley (No. 1)* [1997] 1 All ER 577)	Simple grief (*Vernon* v. *Bosley (No. 1)*)
Personality disorder (*Chadwick* v. *British Railways Board* [1967] 2 All ER 945)	
Miscarriage (*Hay or Bourhill* v. *Young* [1942] 2 All ER 396)	

In addition the psychiatric damage must be caused by a 'sudden event'.

Alcock v. *Chief Constable of South Yorkshire* [1992] 4 All ER 907

Concerning: psychiatric injury; sudden event

Facts

The police allowed a large crowd of football supporters into an already crowded stand which was surrounded by a high perimeter fence. In the chaos that followed, 95 people were crushed to death. A large number of claims were made by those present at the scene and those who had viewed the events on the television. Claims were made by various family members and friends of those present.

Legal principle

Lord Ackner stated that:

> Shock ... involves the sudden appreciation by sight or sound of a horrifying sight or sound or a horrifying event, which violently agitates the mind. It has yet to include psychiatric illness caused by the accumulation over a period of time of more gradual assaults on the nervous system.

The elements of the tort

Since psychiatric injury is a special case of negligence the elements of the tort are the same:

- The defendant owed a duty of care to the claimant
- The defendant breached the duty
- The claimant suffered damage
- The damage was not too remote.

Duty of care

A duty of care is owed if the claimant is a *reasonably foreseeable victim*.

Alcock v. *Chief Constable of South Yorkshire* [1992] 4 All ER 907

Concerning: psychiatric injury claims

Facts

The facts are stated above.

Legal principle

The House of Lords laid down three factors to be considered in determining whether a duty of care is owed in psychiatric injury cases:

KEY CASE

- *Foreseeability* – it must be reasonably foreseeable that a person of normal fortitude in the position of the claimant would suffer illness due to their close ties of love and affection with the victim; *and*
- *Proximity* – there must be temporal and spatial proximity of the claimant in relation to the accident; *and*
- *How the shock was caused.*

The definition of the reasonably foreseeable victim was subsequently considered by the House of Lords in *Page* v. *Smith* [1995] 2 All ER 736:

KEY CASE

Page v. *Smith* [1995] 2 All ER 736

Concerning: psychiatric injury; reasonably foreseeable victim

Facts

The claimant was involved in a road accident with the defendant when the defendant failed to give way when turning out of a side road. The claimant was physically unhurt in the collision, but the accident caused him to suffer the onset of myalgic encephalomyelitis (ME) from which he had suffered for about 20 years but which was then in remission.

Legal principle

The House of Lords held that foreseeability of physical injury was sufficient to allow a claimant directly involved in the incident to recover in psychiatric injury even if physical harm does not occur. In doing so, they identified two types of victim – *primary* and *secondary* victims.

Primary victims

Primary victims are directly involved in the incident.

In *Alcock, rescuers* were also placed in the class of primary victims. However, in *White and Others* v. *Chief Constable of the South Yorkshire Police* [1999] 1 All ER 1, the House of Lords modified the position with regard to rescuers such that they must show actual or apprehended danger – in other words, the rescuer must establish objective exposure to danger or a reasonable belief that there was an exposure to danger.

In *Dooley* v. *Cammell Laird and Co Ltd* [1951] 1 Lloyd's Rep 271 and *Wigg* v. *British Railways Board* (1986) 136 NLJ 446 a further category of primary victims was established in situations where the *claimant believes he has caused another's death or injury.*This would only succeed if the claimant was actually present when the death or injury occurred (*Hunter* v. *British Coal* [1998] 2 All ER 97). However, this category was removed in *White (sub nom Frost) and Others* v. *Chief Constable of South*

Yorkshire Police [1999] 1 All ER 1 where the House of Lords held that only persons in *actual danger of physical harm* can be classified as primary victims.

Secondary victims

Secondary victims must satisfy the tests laid down in *Alcock*:

■ There must be a close relationship of love and affection with the primary victim (there is a rebuttable presumption in favour of this in the case of parents and spouses)

■ Ordinary passers-by *may* be able to claim if the incident witnessed was 'particularly horrific' (although this was unsuccessful in *McFarlane* v. *E E Caledonia Ltd* [1995] 1 Lloyd's Rep 535).

In certain circumstances it may be possible for a claimant to succeed in psychiatric injury after witnessing destruction of property (*Attia* v. *British Gas plc* [1987] 3 All ER 455).

Proximity

The issue of proximity was considered in *McLoughlin* v. *O'Brian* [1982] 2 All ER 298.

KEY CASE

McLoughlin v. *O'Brian* [1982] 2 All ER 298

Concerning: psychiatric injury; spatial and temporal proximity

Facts

The claimant's husband and children were involved in a road accident. The claimant, who was two miles away at the time, was told of the accident about two hours later by a neighbour, who took her to hospital to see her family. There she learnt that her youngest daughter had been killed, and she saw her husband and the other children, and witnessed the nature and extent of their injuries. They were still in the same state as at the scene; covered in oil and mud. The claimant sued in nervous shock.

Legal principle

The nervous shock suffered was the reasonably foreseeable result of the injuries to her family caused by the defendant's negligence and she was entitled to recover damages.

To satisfy the requirement of proximity, the claimant need not be present at the time of the accident, but must come upon the *immediate aftermath*.

How the shock was caused

The claimant must see or hear the event *through unaided sight or hearing*. In *Alcock* it was held that shock communicated by live television broadcasts was not sufficient since it did not show recognisable or identifiable individuals suffering.

Remoteness

Primary victims	Secondary victims
Defendant must or should have foreseen some physical injury to claimant	Psychiatric injury must be foreseeable in a person of reasonable fortitude in the circumstances
Even if no physical injury occurs, but psychiatric injury does, defendant is still liable	

The 'egg-shell skull' rule

The 'egg-shell skull' rule also applies in cases of psychiatric damage. Therefore defendants must take their victims as they find them in respect to psychiatric injury, even if the victims suffer greater injury than a person of reasonable fortitude (*Brice* v. *Brown* [1984] 1 All ER 997).

Chapter summary
Putting it all together

TEST YOURSELF

- [ ] Can you tick all the points from the revision checklist at the beginning of this chapter?
- [ ] Take the **end-of-chapter quiz** on the companion website.
- [ ] Test your knowledge of the cases with the **revision flashcards** on the website.
- [ ] Attempt the problem question from the beginning of the chapter using the guidelines below.
- [ ] Go to the companion website to try out other questions.

Answer guidelines

See the problem question at the start of the chapter. A diagram illustrating how to structure your answer is available on the website.

1 This question concerns liability in negligence for psychiatric harm to both Brenda and Simon. You should deal with each of the parties separately.

2 Who is the defendant? Sid – or his employers under vicarious liability (see Chapter 4).

■ **Brenda**: is her condition medically recognised? Pathological grief is a medically recognised condition (*Vernon* v. *Bosley (No. 1)*).

■ Was her illness caused by a sudden event? The bus crash was a sudden and instantaneous event (*Alcock*).

■ Was she a reasonably foreseeable victim? She was not physically involved in the accident although she did see its aftermath – she is therefore a secondary victim (*Page* v. *Smith*).

■ As she is a secondary victim, she must satisfy the test laid down in *Alcock*.

■ Is there a close relationship of love and affection with the primary victim (Eddie)? Brenda would need to prove this. There is no presumption in favour of grandparents. Eddie had come to visit for the weekend which might suggest that he and Brenda were close. This is not necessarily so – we are not told – Eddie may have been there under orders from his family, or gone there knowing that Brenda was just about to write her will!

■ Did Brenda come upon the immediate aftermath of the accident? The bus was still on fire when she drove past. However, she did not find out about Eddie's death until the morning. This may not be enough to satisfy the requirements of proximity (*McLoughlin* v. *O'Brian*).

■ **Simon**: post-traumatic stress disorder is medically recognised (*Leach* v. *Chief Constable of Gloucestershire*).

■ Rescuers are classed as primary victims if they are exposed to actual or apprehended danger (*White* v. *Chief Constable of South Yorkshire*). Simon rescued people from a burning bus that had just collided with a petrol tanker. This would be likely to satisfy the objective requirement of exposure to danger.

■ The 'egg-shell skull' rule applies to cases of psychiatric damage. Therefore Simon's pre-existing stress condition makes no difference to Sid's defence (*Brice* v. *Brown*).

Make your answer really stand out

■ Don't try to apply the law to the facts of both claims simultaneously. It will lead to a very confused answer, which the marker will struggle to follow.

■ Make sure that you identify each of the relevant points of the law as they relate to the claimants and then apply the law to the facts to reach a reasoned conclusion.

■ Where it is not possible to reach a firm conclusion (for example in the relationship of love and affection between Brenda and Eddie) then put both sides of the argument and assess the relative strengths and weaknesses of both. A well-balanced answer will attract more marks.

4
Vicarious liability

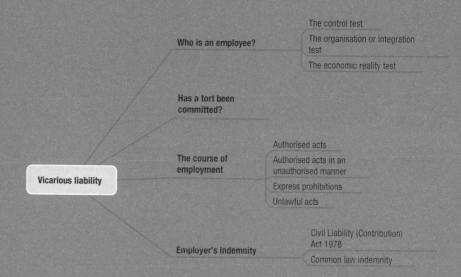

Who is an employee?
- The control test
- The organisation or integration test
- The economic reality test

Has a tort been committed?

The course of employment
- Authorised acts
- Authorised acts in an unauthorised manner
- Express prohibitions
- Unlawful acts

Vicarious liability

Employer's Indemnity
- Civil Liability (Contribution) Act 1978
- Common law indemnity

Revision checklist

What you need to know:

- [ ] The requirements that must be satisfied for vicarious liability to arise
- [ ] The tests used to distinguish between an employee and an independent contractor
- [ ] The meaning of, course of employment, and the relevance of 'a frolic of one's own'
- [ ] The implications of failure to obey instructions or the commission of an intentionally wrongful act
- [ ] The ways in which an employer may recover the cost of paying damages to the claimant from the employee.

Introduction:
Vicarious liability

Vicarious liability is a term used to explain the liability of one person for torts committed by another person.

The general rule is that a person who commits a tort will be personally liable: the claimant brings an action against the person who has caused harm/damage or otherwise fulfilled the requirements of one of the torts that are actionable *per se*. Vicarious liability is an exception to this rule and it gives the claimant the ability to hold someone other than the person who commits the tort liable. It arises most usually in relation to employers and employees and this chapter will focus primarily on that relationship to explain the principles of vicarious liability. It is often advantageous for a claimant to bring an action against an employer on the basis of vicarious liability because there is more likelihood that the employer will be able to pay damages, either personally or under an insurance policy. Vicarious liability is an important revision topic due to the unique way in which it imposes secondary liability on someone not directly involved in the tort. This means that it can combine with any of the other torts covered in this book.

Essay question advice

Vicarious liability is a popular essay topic because it requires students to demonstrate that they have grasped a complicated way of imposing liability on third parties. As it is a strict liability tort, it also raises questions concerning the fairness of imposing liability on employers for torts committed by employees that they could not have prevented.

Problem question advice

Vicarious liability is a popular subject for a problem question and it can combine with any other tort. It is easily overlooked because students focus on the most direct cause of a tort as a potential defendant. Remember that vicarious liability arises most frequently in an employment context so always consider it as a possibility if any tort is committed by someone as part of their employment.

Sample question

Could you answer this question? Below is a typical essay question that could arise on this topic. Guidelines on answering the question are included at the end of the chapter, whilst a sample problem question and guidance on tackling it can be found on the companion website.

Essay question

Vicarious liability represents 'a compromise between two conflicting principles: on the one hand, the social interest in furnishing an innocent tort victim with recourse against a financially responsible defendant; on the other, a hesitation to foist any undue burden on business enterprise'. (Fleming, J.G. (1998) *The Law of Torts*, 9th edn, Sydney: LBC Information Services pp. 409–410).

Discuss the extent to which the case law has maintained a balance between these conflicting principles.

■Vicarious liability

Vicarious liability arises as a result of the relationship between the person who commits the tort and a third party. Although the most common relationship which gives rise to vicarious liability is the employer/employee relationship, there are other relationships of which you should be aware:

- Principal and agent
- Business partners
- Vehicle owners and delegated drivers.

There are three essential components that must be satisfied in order that a third party can be held liable for the torts committed by another. These components are outlined in general terms in Figure 4.1 and also in relation to the employer/employee relationship that forms the main focus of this chapter.

Figure 4.1

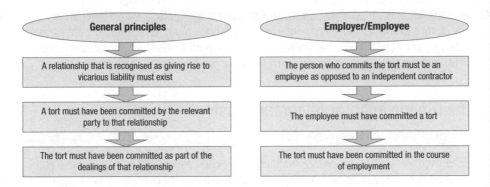

Who is an employee?

An employer is only liable for torts committed by his employees and not those committed by an independent contractor so the distinction between these two is important. Many working relationships fall clearly into the employer/employee relationship such as sales assistants, solicitors and university lecturers whilst others, such as landscape gardeners and electricians, are independent contractors who provide their services to a range of people. However, the distinction is not always clear-cut:

▌ A lecturer may be an independent contractor if, rather than working for a particular university, they provide personal tuition services to students on an individual basis.
▌ An electrician may be an employee if, rather than working on his own account doing lots of different jobs for different people, he works exclusively within one organisation.

The central feature that distinguishes an employee and an independent contractor is not the type of work that they do but the way in which the work is done. The courts have formulated a number of different tests that seek to get to the heart of this distinction.

The control test

KEY DEFINITION

The **control test** distinguishes an employee and an independent contractor on the basis of whether the employer had the right to control the nature of the work done and, most importantly, how it must be done: *Yewen* v. *Noakes* (1880) 6 QBD 530.

This is the oldest test that was used to determine whether a person was an employee and it has its origins in the 'master and servant' nature of the employment relationship. It is an unrealistic way of distinguishing employees and independent contractors in modern employment situations where many employers do not have the expertise or knowledge to supervise the way in which skilled employees carry out their work: imagine an airline company telling a pilot how to fly an aeroplane!

The organisation or integration test

> ### KEY DEFINITION
>
> The **organisation test** makes a distinction between a *contract of service* whereby 'a man is employed as part of the business and his work is done as an integral part of the business' and a *contract for services* whereby 'work, although done for the business, is not integrated into it but is only accessory to it': *Stevenson, Jordan and Harrison Ltd* v. *Macdonald and Evans* [1952] 1 TLR 101.

The distinction between a contract *of* service and a contract *for* services can be hard to grasp. The explanation and example given in the table below may help you to understand the difference.

Contract of service	Contract for services
An organisation engages a person to carry out various tasks within the organisation that are integral to its core purpose	An organisation requires a particular service to be supplied and seeks out a person who can provide that service, which is supplementary to the core purpose of the organisation
e.g. An organisation that produces components for domestic electrical goods employs an electrician to carry out safety checks on the finished products	e.g. An organisation that produces double glazing products engages an electrician to rewire the factory

The economic reality test

In recognition that the control and organisation/integration tests do not cover all situations in which it is necessary to determine whether someone is an employee or an independent contractor, the courts developed the economic reality test (sometimes called the 'multiple test' or the 'pragmatic test'):

Ready Mixed Concrete Ltd v. *Minister of Pensions* [1968] 2 QB 497

Concerning: employees; economic reality test

Facts

Drivers were hired by the claimant organisation to deliver concrete using vehicles owned by the drivers which they purchased from the claimant and which had to be painted the company colours and carry the company logo. Drivers were responsible for the maintenance of the vehicles and had flexible hours of work. It was held that the drivers were not employees thus the claimant was not liable for their national insurance contributions.

Legal principle

It was held that there were three conditions that had to be met before a worker would be considered to be an employee:

1 The employee must provide work or skill for the employer in return for payment of a wage or some other remuneration.
2 The employee agrees, expressly or impliedly, that they will work under the control of the employer.
3 All other circumstances are consistent with the situation being characterised as a contract of employment.

The first two requirements should be relatively easy to ascertain, whereas the third is an extremely open provision that could cover the following points:

- **Method of payment**: employees tend to receive regular payments (weekly, monthly) whereas contractors are more likely to receive a lump sum for a particular piece of work;
- **Tax and National Insurance**: employees usually have deductions made at source, i.e. by the employer, whereas independent contractors are responsible for their own contributions;
- **Working hours**: employees often have fixed or regulated hours of work whereas independent contractors are more likely to set their own schedule of work;
- **Provision of equipment**: an employee will expect an employer to provide an equipped working environment with the tools needed to complete their duties whereas an independent contractor will usually provide their own tools and equipment;
- **Level of independence**: employees are generally quite constrained in the scope of their duties whilst independent contractors have more control, particularly in terms of working for more than one person and in being able to refuse to carry out certain tasks or to reject work altogether.

EXAM TIP

No single test is accepted as authoritative by the courts although it is the economic reality test that tends to be applied as it covers aspects of both of the other tests. In any essay, you might want to consider how these tests have evolved and address whether they provide a reliable means for distinguishing employees and independent contractors. In a problem question, you will need to apply the economic reality test to determine whether someone is an employee, remembering to take into account the factors listed above in deciding the third limb of the *Ready Mixed Concrete* test.

Has a tort been committed?

This second requirement for vicarious liability is often overlooked. This is essential as there can be no vicarious (secondary) liability if there is no direct (primary) liability. In other words, if the employee does not satisfy the requirements of a tort, the employer cannot be held vicariously liable.

REVISION NOTE

It is often the case that the relevant tort is negligence so make sure that you have a good grasp of this topic. However, vicarious liability can apply to any tort so it might be useful to remind yourself of the key principles of the various torts that you have studied and think about how these could occur in an employer/employee relationship.

If the employee has committed a criminal offence, this may give rise to liability if the elements of a tort were also satisfied. For example, an employee who attacks a customer will also have satisfied the requirements of the tort of battery so the situation may give rise to vicarious liability.

The course of employment

An employer is not liable for all torts committed by an employee, only those which take place during the course of employment.

KEY DEFINITION

A **frolic of his own** is a phrase used to describe conduct that falls outside of the course of employment because it is something that the employee has done within working time that is unrelated to his work and is undertaken on his own account: *Joel* v. *Morrison* (1834) 6 C&P 501. For example, a delivery driver who deviates from his authorised route to visit a friend in hospital will be on a frolic of his own as this is a 'new and independent journey … entirely for his own business': *Storey* v. *Ashton* (1869) LR 4 QB 476.

Rather than the timing or location of the employment, it is accepted that course of employment is more concerned with the duties of the employment: what the employee is employed to do. There are two situations which are accepted as falling within the scope of course of employment:

■ Acts by the employee that are authorised by the employer
■ Acts which, although not authorised by the employer, are so closely connected with what the employee was supposed to be doing that they can be considered as carrying out an authorised act in an unauthorised, or wrongful, manner.

Authorised acts

This category is straightforward. If the employee is following his employer's instructions and commits a tort in doing so, the employer will be vicariously liable. For example, if a security guard is told to detain a suspected shoplifter, the employer will be vicariously liable if this results in battery or false imprisonment (see Chapter 9).

Authorised acts in an unauthorised manner

This covers a range of situations such as acting contrary to instructions or performing an authorised task in a negligent manner.

KEY CASE

Century Insurance v. *NI Road Transport Board* [1942] AC 509

Concerning: authorised acts in an unauthorised manner

Facts

The driver was employed to deliver petrol which involved transferring the petrol from his lorry to a storage tank at his destination. Whilst doing so, he lit a cigarette and threw the match on the ground, causing an explosion.

Legal principle

It was held that the driver was acting in the course of his employment. He was doing exactly what he was supposed to be doing (delivering petrol) albeit in a woefully careless manner.

This can be distinguished from situations in which the employee does something which is beyond the scope of his employment responsibilities, even if he is acting from good motives:

Beard v. *London Omnibus Co* [1990] 2 QB 530

Concerning: acts beyond the scope of employment

Facts

A bus conductor drove a bus around the front of the bus depot as he knew that it was needed urgently for its next journey and the driver could not be found. Whilst manoeuvring the bus, the conductor injured a mechanic.

Legal principle

It was no part of the conductor's duties to drive the bus thus in doing so he was outside of the course of his employment. As such, the employer was not vicariously liable for the injury caused to the mechanic.

EXAM TIP

A useful way to identify whether the employee is acting within the course of employment is to ask the question, 'what is this person employed to do?'. As you see in *Century Insurance*, doing the tasks that you are supposed to do, even to a poor standard or in a dangerous manner, will usually fall within the course of employment.

Express prohibitions

If an employer has explicitly prohibited an employee from acting in a particular manner or taking on a certain task, you might expect that acting contrary to these

Figure 4.2

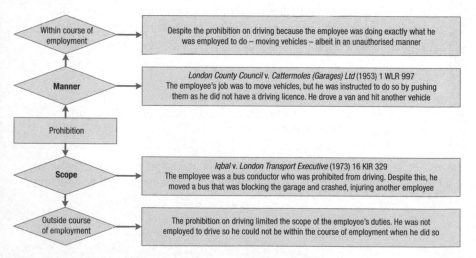

instructions would take the employee outside of the course of employment. However, this is not always the case as the courts have made a distinction between prohibitions relating to the *manner* (how the employee should do the job) and *scope* (what the employee should do) of employment. See Figure 4.2.

Unlawful acts

You might expect that the deliberate commission of a criminal act by an employee would automatically take him outside the course of his employment but this is not necessarily the case. The courts have developed a test to determine whether an employer will be vicariously liable for intentional wrongful acts of employees:

KEY CASE

Lister and others v. *Hesley Hall Ltd* [2001] 2 All ER 769

Concerning: intentional wrongful acts

Facts

The claimants were residential students at a school for difficult children owned by the defendant. One of the wardens employed by the defendant was sexually abusing the children in his care and was eventually subjected to criminal proceedings. The claimants sought to hold the defendant vicariously liable for the harms they suffered as a result of the abuse.

Legal principle

The House of Lords adopted the 'closeness of connection' to determine whether an intentionally wrongful act by an employee would fall within the course of employment. Here, the sexual abuse occurred on the employer's premises whilst the employee was engaged in performing his duties of caring for the children. As such, there was a close connection between the employment and the abuse so the employer would be vicariously liable. This was particularly so as there was an obvious risk of sexual abuse in the circumstances so the employer should have been alert for it.

The closeness of connection test requires an assessment of the link between the employee's wrongful act and the tasks that he was supposed to be carrying out. This picks up on the established position of finding vicarious liability if the situation can be characterised as an unauthorised way of carrying out an authorised task.

Close connection	No connection
An employee responsible for conveyancing in a firm of solicitors fraudulently induces an elderly client to sign documents that pass ownership of her properties to him (*Lloyd* v. *Green Smith & Co* [1912] AC 716). This was within the course of employment as it was a dishonest way of doing the tasks that the employee was engaged to carry out.	A secretary employed by a firm of solicitor took advantage of the knowledge she had picked up to pose as a solicitor to a new client. She prepared papers for him to sign, one of which gave her authority to access his bank account. She transferred £100,000 to her own account. This would not fall within the course of employment as there was no connection between her actions and her responsibilities as a secretary.
A security guard rugby-tackles a shoplifter to stop them leaving the supermarket with stolen goods. In doing so, he is performing the task that he is engaged to do, i.e. protect the employer's property, so is acting within the course of his employment.	An estate agent punches a colleague upon discovering he has been having an affair with his wife. This has no link with his employment as an estate agent so will not give rise to vicarious liability.

FURTHER THINKING

The test formulated in *Lister* has implications for vicarious liability in that it imposed liability on an 'innocent' employer for the intentional criminal acts of an employee. You might find it useful to read the House of Lords decision for insight into the policy underlying the decision. The following article also provides a detailed analysis of the decision and would make useful reading in preparation for an essay:

Roe, R., '*Lister* v. *Helsey Hall*' (2002) *Modern Law Review* vol. 65, 270

Employer's indemnity

As vicarious liability only arises if the employee has committed a tort, the employer and employee are regarded as joint tortfeasors. This means that the employer may be able to recover some of the cost of paying damages to the claimant from the employee. There are two ways in which this could occur, detailed below.

Civil Liability (Contribution) Act 1978

Section 1(1) allows a defendant who has paid damages to a claimant to recover a contribution from any other defendant who is responsible for the harm or loss caused (whether liability is joint or several).

The quantification of the contribution is decided on the basis of what is 'just and equitable' in the circumstances of the case, section 2(1), but could cover the whole amount of damages paid to the claimant if the court felt that the employer, although vicariously liable for the employee's tort, was entirely blameless.

KEY DEFINITIONS

Joint liability arises if two or more people cause harm/damage to the same claimant when they are (1) engaged in a joint enterprise (the author and publisher of a defamatory article); (2) one party authorises the tort of the other (A tells B to park his car on C's land); and (3) one party is vicariously liable for the torts of the other (employer/employee).

Several liability occurs in all other cases that do not fall within these three categories but where more than one defendant has caused harm/damage to the claimant. For example, if a collision between two vehicles damaged the claimant's wall, the drivers would be severally liable.

Common law indemnity

In *Lister* v. *Romford Ice & Cold Storage Co Ltd* [1957] 1 All ER 125, the House of Lords held that an employer could obtain an indemnity (the full cost of the damages paid to the claimant) if the loss or injury had been caused by the employee's breach of contract (in this case, breach of the implied duty to exercise reasonable care and skill).

An employer cannot claim an indemnity at common law unless he is in no way to blame for the employee's conduct: *Jones* v. *Manchester Corporation* [1952] 2 All ER 125.

EXAM TIP

In a question involving vicarious liability, do not forget to consider whether the employer can recover some or all of the damages paid to the claimant from the employee. It is worth mentioning the possibility of indemnity under *Lister* but requirement of faultlessness is likely to make recovery under the statutory scheme preferable.

Chapter summary:
Putting it all together

TEST YOURSELF

- [ ] Can you tick all the points from the revision checklist at the beginning of this chapter?
- [ ] Take the **end-of-chapter quiz** on the companion website.
- [ ] Test your knowledge of the cases with the **revision flashcards** on the website.
- [ ] Attempt the essay question from the beginning of the chapter using the guidelines below.
- [ ] Go to the companion website to try out other questions.

Answer guidelines

See the essay question at the start of the chapter. A diagram illustrating how to structure your answer is available on the website.

1 Remember that there is credit available for doing simple things well. Your answer should include a concise explanation of vicarious liability which will form a basis for the rest of the answer. It would also be useful to 'unpick' the quotation a little, explaining the way in which the employee has caused the harm for which the employer may be liable hence vicarious liability is a means of determining which of two innocent parties (the employer and the claimant) should suffer.

2 Take time to plan a structure for the answer. There are two opposing viewpoints to discuss; do you want to separate the essay into two sections addressing these views or would it be preferable to identify a list of points and consider each from the two viewpoints?

3 The question requires an examination of how case law balances these two interests so you will need to select cases which seem to take one or the other position as priority as well as those in which the interests are more evenly balanced.

4 Make sure that you do not lose the focus of the question. It is always tempting to include pieces of information that you can remember that are related to vicarious liability but this will not attract any credit unless they are relevant to the question. For example, there is no scope here for a discussion of the tests that distinguish an employee and an independent contractor other than to comment that tests which favour a finding that a worker is an employee increase the reach of vicarious liability.

Make your answer really stand out

■ You could look beyond case law to consider some of the principles that determine whether or not an employer will be vicariously liable for the torts of his employee. For example, do you think that the distinction between prohibitions on manner and scope strike an appropriate balance between the interests of the employer and that of the claimant?

■ Remember that evidence of wide reading will attract credit from the examiners. Include journal articles on key issues in your revision and try to incorporate these into your essays. There will be case notes published on recent developments, particularly House of Lords decisions, which will help you to engage in more detailed analysis. In relation to this question, the ability to comment on *Lister* v. *Hesley Hall* would be particularly advantageous.

5
Employers' liability

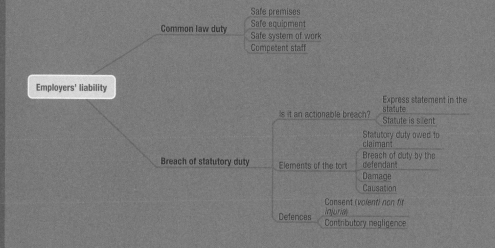

Employers' liability

Common law duty
- Safe premises
- Safe equipment
- Safe system of work
- Competent staff

Breach of statutory duty

Is it an actionable breach?
- Express statement in the statute
- Statute is silent

Elements of the tort
- Statutory duty owed to claimant
- Breach of duty by the defendant
- Damage
- Causation

Defences
- Consent (*volenti non fit injuria*)
- Contributory negligence

Revision checklist

What you need to know:

- [ ] The scope of the common law duty to ensure the safety of employees
- [ ] The operation of the law in relation to safety of premises, plant, system of work and competency of staff
- [ ] The elements of the tort of breach of statutory duty
- [ ] The tests used to determine whether a breach is actionable.

Introduction:
Employers' liability

Employers' liability covers a range of statutory and common law duties placed upon an employer in order to protect employees against injury at work.

There is a fair degree of overlap between the common law protection which has developed over many years and the statutory protection introduced by key legislation such as the Health and Safety at Work Act 1974. An employer may also be vicariously liable for an injury caused by one employee to another (see Chapter 4). This is an area of law that has been strongly influenced by an influx of European law aimed at ensuring that all member states have high levels of industrial safety.

There are approximately 500,000 injuries in the workplace every year and around 10% of those injured at work attempt to rely on tort law to obtain compensation.

Essay question advice

The range of sources of an employer's duty to his employees makes this an unpopular topic with students and its popularity with examiners fluctuates so check your syllabus to see how much attention was given to this topic during your course.

Problem question advice

Employers' liability often combines with vicarious liability in a problem question so it is important that you are familiar with both topics.

Sample question

Could you answer this question? Below is a typical problem question that could arise on this topic. Guidelines on answering the question are included at the end of the chapter, whilst a sample essay question and guidance on tackling it can be found on the companion website.

Problem question

Christine was employed by FruitInc, a company specialising in the canning of fresh fruit, as a canning machine operator. The machine had sharp moving parts which are required to be fenced by section 14(1) of the Factories Act 1961:

> Every dangerous part of any machinery ... shall be securely fenced.

FruitInc had secured a guard fence around the moving parts of the canning machine with a sign stating that 'This guard must not be removed except by a Manager'.

Christine (who was not a manager) removed the guard. David, the manager, noticed that the guard had been removed but did nothing. That afternoon, Christine caught her hair in the machine and was scalped, suffering severe head injuries as a result.

Advise Christine if she has any claims in tort against FruitInc.

■ Common law duty

An employer has a common law duty to take reasonable care to ensure the safety of his employees. This is a personal and non-delegable duty which means that the employer cannot escape liability by claiming to have passed the responsibility for the employee's safety to another party, i.e. an independent contractor. For example, if an employee was injured in a workplace fire caused by faulty wiring that had been installed by an independent contractor, the employer would not be able to pass liability on to them.

Employers' liability reflects the ordinary principles of negligence in that only injuries that have been sustained by a failure to take reasonable care will give rise to liability. The duty was said in *Wilsons & Clyde Coal Co Ltd* v. *English* [1937] 3 All ER 628 to cover four key elements:

- The duty to provide safe premises and a safe place to work
- The duty to provide safe plant, materials and equipment
- The duty to provide a safe system of work and safe working practices
- The duty to provide a competent staff as colleagues.

Safe premises

The duty to provide safe premises is concerned with the building itself and structural aspects of it such as the floors (*Latimer* v. *AEC*) below and windows (*General Cleaning Contractors* v. *Christmas* [1953] AC 180) so as to distinguish it from the plant and machinery within the building (safe equipment) and the way that the work is done within the building (safe system of work). The employer must take reasonable steps to ensure that the employee is not injured by defective premises:

KEY CASE

Latimer v. *AEC Ltd* [1953] AC 643

Concerning: reasonable care

Facts

A factory floor was dangerously slippery following flooding. The employer put down sawdust but did not have enough to cover the whole floor. The employee was injured when he slipped on an uncovered patch.

Legal principle

There would be no liability as the employer had done what was reasonable in the circumstances to protect against the particular risk.

If the employee's work takes him onto premises owned by others, the employer must take reasonable steps to ensure that these are safe and will not injure his employee. In *Cook* v. *Square D Ltd* [1992] ACR 262, the Court of Appeal identified the factors that an employer must consider when determining whether a workplace is safe for an employee:

- The location where the work is required to be done
- The nature of the building
- The nature of the work required from the employee
- The employee's expertise and experience
- The degree of control that it is reasonable to expect the employer to exercise
- Whether the employer is aware that the premises are dangerous.

Safe equipment

The employer must provide safe and appropriate equipment and ensure that it is properly maintained. This duty is supplemented by the Employers' Liability (Defective Equipment) Act 1969 which defines 'equipment' as 'any plant and machinery, vehicle, aircraft and clothing' and expands the duty upon the employer to include liability for equipment that is defective due to the negligence of third parties, i.e. the manufacturer.

KEY CASE

Knowles v. Liverpool County Council [1994] 1 Lloyd's Rep 11

Concerning: liability for existing defects

Facts

The claimant injured his finger when a flagstone that he was carrying broke due to an inherent defect in its manufacture. The employer argued (1) that he could not have known about the defect so should not be liable and (2) that a flagstone was not equipment.

Legal principle

The House of Lords held that section 1(1)(b) of the Employers' Liability (Defective Equipment) Act 1969 made it clear that the employer would be liable for defects that were not obvious or visible and which were caused by a third party such as a manufacturer. Further, the broad definition of 'equipment' would encompass 'any article of whatever kind furnished by the employer for the purposes of his business'.

Although the duty is broad, liability may be avoided (as with all categories of duty) if the employer can establish that the defective equipment did not cause the employee's injury. For example, if the employer can establish that the employee would not have used safety equipment even if it had been provided, he will not be liable: *McWilliams* v. *Sir William Arrol & Co Ltd* [1962] 1 WLR 295.

Safe system of work

This is the area that gives rise to the greatest number of claims. Case law has elaborated on the elements covered by a safe system of work:

Speed v. *Thomas Swift & Co Ltd* [1943] 1 KB 557

Concerning: safe system of work

Facts

The claimant was injured during the loading of a ship because there were several deficiencies with the system used to do so and the ship in question was not suited to the usual routine used for loading.

Legal principle

The court considered that the duty to provide a safe system of work included four features:

(1) The physical layout of the job.
(2) The sequence by which the work is carried out.
(3) The provision of warnings and notices and the issue of special instructions where necessary.
(4) The need to modify or improve the system to respond to particular circumstances.

The following situations are covered by the requirement to provide a safe system of work:

■ Failing to warn employees of the dangers associated with their work: *Pape* v. *Cumbria County Council* [1992] 3 All ER 211 (the employer did not tell cleaners that failing to use gloves when handing chemicals could lead to dermatitis)
■ Failing to ensure that safety measures provided were used: *Bux* v. *Slough Metals* [1974] 1 All ER 262 (the employer knew that the employee refused to wear safety goggles provided but did nothing, thus was liable when his eyes were injured by molten metal)
■ Failing to take action to guard against known risks: *Rahman* v. *Arearose Ltd* [2000] 3 WLR 1184 (the employer was liable when his employee was attacked by a customer as he had taken no action to introduce a system to prevent this despite attacks against other members of staff in the past)
■ Failure to protect against psychiatric injury: *Walker* v. *Northumberland County Council* [1995] 1 All ER 737 (the employer did nothing to alter an employee's workload after he returned to work following a nervous breakdown, thus was liable when he suffered a second breakdown as they were aware he was susceptible to stress).

Competent staff

The employer must ensure that he recruits competent staff and that an appropriate level of training and supervision is provided to ensure that employees do not pose a threat to the safety of their colleagues.

This category of duty overlaps with vicarious liability (Chapter 4) thus giving an employee injured by a colleague two potential ways of holding the employer liable (in addition to the personal liability of the colleague responsible); see Figure 5.1.

Figure 5.1

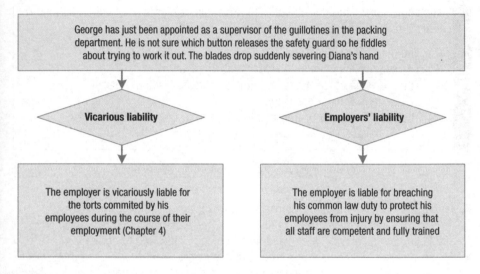

■ Breach of statutory duty

The common law duty is supplemented by statute law which imposes further duties on employers. The most commonly encountered statutory duties arise from the *Health and Safety at Work etc. Act 1974* although there are others. Claims for breach of statutory duty therefore most commonly arise in the context of employment. If an employer breaches his statutory duty and this results in injury to the employee, then this may give rise to a civil claim.

Is it an actionable breach?

Not all statutes give rise to a civil claim if breached.

Express statement in the statute

A few statutes expressly state that a claim in tort will be allowed if they are breached including:

- Consumer Protection Act 1987
- Misrepresentation Act 1967
- Mineral Workings (Offshore Installations) Act 1971.

Statute is silent

However, most statutes are silent as to whether an action in tort arises in the event of a breach. The courts will first look to see if there has been a precedent set in case law deciding the issue of civil liability.

If there is no precedent the court will consider a range of factors in deciding Parliament's intention in enacting the statute. Most importantly, if the statute was designed to protect a limited class of individuals then it is more likely that a claim in tort will be allowed.

KEY CASE

Lonrho Ltd v. Shell Petroleum Co Ltd (No 2) [1982] AC 173

Concerning: breach of statute giving rise to civil liability

Facts

A sanctions order made under the Southern Rhodesia Act 1965 prohibited anyone from supplying or delivering any crude oil or petroleum products to Southern Rhodesia on a penalty of a fine or imprisonment. The appellants argued that contravention of the sanctions order would amount to breach of statutory duty by the respondents giving the appellants a right of action in tort.

Legal principle

Lord Diplock stated that the test for deciding whether a statute gives rise to civil liability is that:

> ... the court should presume that if the Act creates an obligation which is enforceable in a specific manner then it is not enforceable in any other manner. In this way if the Act was intended for the general benefit of the community rather than for the granting of individual rights then it will not usually be possible to use the Act to bring an action in tort.

The exceptions to this rule are:

- Where the Act benefits a particular class of individuals
- Where the claimant suffered damage which was particular, direct and substantial and different from that suffered by the rest of the public.

The courts will also look to see whether the statute provides a remedy for its breach. If the statute providing protection to a limited class of individuals provides no remedy for its breach then the courts are likely to infer that Parliament intended for a civil claim to lie – otherwise those protected by the statute would have no remedy at all in respect of the protection that the statute offered (*Cutler* v. *Wandsworth Stadium Ltd* [1949] AC 398).

Where the statute provides for compensation, this does not automatically mean that this is the only remedy available (*Groves* v. *Lord Wimborne* [1898] All ER Rep 147).

In essence there are many factors which allow the courts discretion in determining whether a right of action in tort will lie for breach of statutory duty. As Lord Simonds said in *Cutler* v. *Wandsworth Stadium Ltd* [1949] AC 398:

> The only rule which in all circumstances is valid is that the answer must depend on a consideration of the whole Act and the circumstances, including the pre-existing law, in which it was enacted.

Elements of the tort

Assuming that the statute allows a civil claim, the claimant must establish the elements of the tort as follows:

- Statutory duty owed to the claimant
- Breach of duty by the defendant
- Damage
- Causation.

Statutory duty owed to the claimant

If the statute protects a limited class of people, then the claimant must establish that they are a member of that class.

KEY CASE

***Hartley* v. *Mayoh & Co.* [1954] 1 QB 383**

Concerning: existence of stautory duty

Facts

The defendants were in breach of the Factory and Workshop Acts 1901, 1907 and 1908 by negligently miswiring electrical switches at a factory. A fireman, called to a fire at the factory, was electrocuted.

Legal principle

The claim, brought by the deceased fireman's widow, failed. The fireman was

---

KEY CASE outside the protected class, since the statutes protected factory workers, not visitors to the factory.

Breach of duty by the defendant

The claimant must establish that the defendant was in breach of duty. This is determined by the wording of the relevant statute.

Some statutes impose *strict liability*. That is to say that the statute will impose an absolute requirement which, if unmet, will be a breach of duty even if the breach is not the defendant's fault.

KEY CASE

John Summers & Sons Ltd v. *Frost* [1955] AC 740

Concerning: breach of statutory duty; strict liability

Facts

The claimant, a maintenance fitter, was employed by the defendants in a steel works. While working on a power-driven grinding machine, his thumb came into contact with the revolving grindstone and he was injured. He brought an action for damages for breach of statutory duty under section 14(1) of the Factories Act 1937.

Legal principle

The Act provided that 'Every dangerous part of any machinery, other than prime movers and transmission machinery, shall be securely fenced ...'. The defendants argued that it would be impracticable to fence their machinery. However, the House of Lords refused to accept this. Liability was strict.

However, the required standard of care may not be stated so precisely. For instance in *Brown* v. *NCB* [1962] AC 574 the duty imposed was 'to take such steps as may be necessary for keeping the road or working place secure'.

EXAM TIP

Problem questions involving breach of statutory duty will usually provide statements from the statute at issue. If liability is not strict, remember to argue both for and against liability being imposed and identify the strengths and weaknesses of both sides. The best answers always show a balanced understanding of all potential outcomes.

Damage

The damage suffered by the claimant must be of the type which the statute was intended to protect.

This requirement is similar to that of remoteness in negligence. Refer back to Chapter 2 to refresh your memory.

KEY CASE

Gorris v. *Scott* (1874) LR 9 Exch 125

Concerning: breach of statutory duty; type of damage

Facts

The defendant, a ship-owner, undertook to carry the claimant's sheep from a foreign port to England. On the voyage some of the sheep were washed overboard by reason of the defendant's failure to take a precaution made under section 75 of the Contagious Diseases (Animals) Act 1869.

Legal principle

The Act was designed to prevent the loss of livestock through contagious diseases. Since the loss suffered was different, the claim did not succeed.

Causation

The final element in the tort is that there must be a causal link between the defendant's breach of duty and the claimant's loss. Where the breach of statutory duty is not the only cause of the defendant's injuries, it is enough that it materially contributed to it (*Bonnington Castings* v. *Wardlaw* [1956] AC 613).

Bonnington Castings v. *Wardlaw* was covered in Chapter 2. It involved a breach of the statutory duty under the Grinding of Metals (Miscellaneous Industries) Regulations 1925 to keep the ducts of dust-extraction plants free from obstruction.

Defences

An employer could seek to limit or avoid liability by relying on the defences of:

■ Consent (*volenti non fit injuria*)
■ Contributory negligence.

Consent

The defence of consent is not available to an employer who is in breach of his own statutory duty. This is a matter of public policy (*Wheeler* v. *New Merton Board Mills Ltd* [1933] 2 KB 669).

However, consent *is* available where an employee sues an employer for being vicariously liable for a colleague's breach of statutory duty (*ICI Ltd* v. *Shatwell* [1964] 2 All ER 999).

With the exceptions above in mind, the defence of consent will be generally available where there has been a breach of statutory duty (Lord Reid in *ICI Ltd* v. *Shatwell*).

Contributory negligence

Contributory negligence is generally available. However, in relation to factory workers, the courts are more reluctant to find contributory negligence against an employee (*Caswell* v. *Powell Duffryn Associated Collieries Ltd* [1940] AC 152).

REVISION NOTE

Contributory negligence and *volenti non fit injuria* (consent) are general defences which are available to most torts in addition to breach of statutory duty. You will find a more detailed outline of the elements of these defences and their operation in Chapter 11.

Chapter summary:
Putting it all together

TEST YOURSELF

- [ ] Can you tick all the points from the revision checklist at the beginning of this chapter?
- [ ] Take the **end-of-chapter quiz** on the companion website.
- [ ] Test your knowledge of the cases with the **revision flashcards** on the website.
- [ ] Attempt the problem question from the beginning of the chapter using the guidelines below.
- [ ] Go to the companion website to try out other questions.

Answer guidelines

See the problem question at the start of the chapter. A diagram illustrating how to structure your answer is available on the website.

This question raises three potential claims against FruitInc. You should deal with each of them in turn.

1 **Common law negligence** – FruitInc has a common law duty to take reasonable care of its employees. It covers four key elements: safe premises/workplace; safe plant, materials and equipment; safe system of work; competent colleagues (*Wilsons & Clyde Coal*). Consider each of these elements in turn.
   ■ Safe workplace? More concerned with building. Probably does not apply here (*Latimer* v. *AEC Ltd*).
   ■ Safe plant? Again, the machine was not unsafe *per se* (*Knowles* v. *Liverpool County Council*).
   ■ Safe system of work? FruitInc has a duty to ensure that the safety measures provided were used (*Speed* v. *Thomas Swift & Co Ltd*; *Bux* v. *Slough Metals*) – probable breach here.
   ■ Competent staff? David was incompetent in not requiring Christine to use the guard.
   FruitInc appears to be in breach of its common law duty of care. Causation is established via the 'but for' test. Christine's injury is a reasonably foreseeable type and therefore not too remote.
   ■ Defences? Consent may work since Christine deliberately removed the guard. If this fails, then contributory negligence is likely to succeed (see Chapter 11).

2 **Breach of statutory duty** – will be allowed if the Factories Act 1961 allows a civil claim. This will be established by reading the Act. If it is silent, as most are, then the next step is looking to see if there is decided case law on the issue. If none, then the court will look at the Act as a whole and decide (*Cutler* v. *Wandsworth Stadium*). This Act appears to protect a limited class of individuals and seems to provide no remedy for its breach. The courts also tend to allow civil claims for breaches of health and safety legislations. It is likely that the Act will allow a claim in tort for a breach of section 14(1).
   ■ Is Christine a member of the protected class? She is a factory worker and is therefore protected (*Hartley* v. *Mayoh & Co*).
   ■ Has there been a breach of duty by FruitInc? Section 14(1) imposes strict liability; hence FruitInc is in breach (*John Summers & Sons Ltd* v. *Frost*).
   ■ Has Christine suffered the type of injury the Act was designed to prevent? Clearly! (*Gorris* v. *Scott*).
   ■ Is there a causal link? But for FruitInc's breach, Christine would not have been scalped.
   ■ Defences? (see Chapter 12). Consent will not be available to FruitInc for a breach of its own statutory duty (*Wheeler* v. *New Merton Board Mills Ltd*).

Contributory negligence is likely to succeed as Christine seemed to recklessly disregard her own safety (but see *Caswell* v. *Powell Duffryn Associated Collieries Ltd*).

3 **Vicarious liability** – (see Chapter 4). FruitInc may be vicariously liable for David's negligence committed in the course of employment which caused Christine's injury of a reasonable foreseeable type. Consent will again be unlikely to succeed, but contributory negligence will be applicable as in the other heads of claim.

Make your answer really stand out

▮ Remember to cover all three potential claims. Don't be misled by the fact that the problem states a statute into only covering breach of statutory duty.

▮ Take each of the claims in turn and analyse them methodically. Remember to relate each point back to the facts and provide supporting case authority for each point of law you make.

6
Occupiers' liability

Occupiers' liability

Occupiers' Liability Act
1957

- Who is an occupier?
- What are premises?
- Who is a visitor?
  - Those with express permission
  - Those with implied permission
  - Those with a right to enter
- Duty of care
  - Children
  - Skilled visitors
- Warning signs
- Liability for independent contractors
- Defences

Occupiers' Liability Act
1984

- Who is a trespasser?
- Duty of care
- Signs and defences

Revision checklist

What you need to know:

- [ ] The meaning of key terms such as occupier, visitor, premises and trespasser
- [ ] The scope of the duty established under the Occupiers' Liability Act 1957
- [ ] The implications of the Occupiers' Liability Act 1984 in relation to liability for trespassers
- [ ] The defences available to an occupier and the ability to limit or exclude liability
- [ ] Liability for dangers created by independent contractors on land occupied by others.

Introduction:
Occupiers' liability

Occupiers have an obligation to ensure that their land is not hazardous to others.

This obligation is governed by statute law as the Occupiers' Liability Act 1957 (OLA 1957) was introduced to clarify the common law position. It was supplemented by the Occupiers' Liability Act 1984 (OLA 1984) which covers injuries caused to trespassers. Occupiers' liability is an important topic because the scope of the tort is so immense; think of all the situations in which you enter land or premises belonging to others: shops, university, pubs, the gym and even friends' houses. All occupiers have a duty to ensure that you are not injured on their land and that your property is not damaged. The statutes should form the central focus of your revision and it is essential that you are able to identify and explain the key provisions that govern liability in this area.

Essay question advice

As with any statute introduced to tackle a particular problem, there is scope for essays that require examination of how well the law has achieved its purpose; in other words, whether the statutes achieve an appropriate level of protection for visitors and trespassers without unduly burdening the occupier of land. Alternatively, essays might explore the necessity for the legislation in light of the protection offered by other areas of tort law such as trespass, nuisance and negligence.

Occupiers' liability is a popular subject for a problem question. It is common for students to overlook this tort and tackle questions on the basis of general principles of negligence so be sure to avoid this pitfall by thorough revision and remaining alert for injury that occurs on another's land which should trigger a discussion of occupiers' liability. It is also essential that the correct statute is applied, so pay careful attention to the distinction between lawful visitors and trespassers.

Sample question

Could you answer this question? Below is a typical problem question that could arise on this topic. Guidelines on answering the question are included at the end of the chapter, whilst a sample essay question and guidance on tackling it can be found on the companion website.

Omar runs a small museum specialising in agricultural artefacts. There are several signs displayed prominently that read 'please do not touch the exhibits' and two of the rarest machines are also roped off to protect them from the public. Lew (4) climbs on an antique plough whilst his mother is queueing in the tea shop. He slips and sustains a deep laceration to his leg from the exposed blades. There is an exhibition of dairy equipment in the cellar which attracts Maggie. She sees that there is a sign at the top of the step but does not put on her glasses to read what it says so she is not aware that part of the handrail is missing. She starts to descend the stairs, slips and falls, breaking her leg. Lucy works in the newly-refurbished tea shop, which was fitted by Bob, a local handyman. Bob struggled with some of the wiring, not being experienced with electrical work, and this causes a power surge during which the coffee machine explodes, causing Lucy to suffer severe burns.

Advise Omar as to the strength of the claims against him.

■Occupiers' Liability Act 1957

Prior to this statute, the extent of liability owed by an occupier depended upon the nature of the relationship with the person injured. The OLA 1957 abolished this in favour of two categories:

■ Lawful visitors, who were protected by the Act
■ All others, who were not protected (most of these are now protected by OLA 1984).

KEY STATUTORY PROVISION

Occupiers' Liability Act 1957, section 1(1)

The purpose of the Act is to 'regulate the duty which an occupier of premises owes to his visitors in respect of dangers due to the state of the premises or to things done or omitted to be done on them'.

Who is an occupier?

There is no statutory definition of 'occupier' thus recourse must be made to the common law which has taken a broad view of the issue:

KEY DEFINITIONS

An **occupier** is a person who exercises an element of control over premises: *Wheat* v. *E. Lacon & Co Ltd* [1966] 1 All ER 582.

■ As there are varying degrees of control that can be exercised, this means that there can be more than one occupier.
■ This includes physical control of premises and legal control of premises; in *Harris* v. *Birkenhead Corporation* [1976] 1 All ER 341, the council was the occupier of an empty house even though it had not taken physical possession as it had served a notice of compulsory purchase on the owner thus was in legal control of the property.

EXAM TIP

Remember that liability falls upon the *occupier* of land and that this may not necessarily be the person who owns the land. The central question is 'who has control of these premises?' and you should also keep in mind that there may be more than one occupier simultaneously.

What are premises?

The definition of premises is wide and covers not only land and buildings but also 'any fixed or moveable structure, including any vessel, vehicle or aircraft': section s1 (3) (a) OLA 1957. This has covered:

■ Ship in dry dock: *London Graving Dock* v. *Horton* [1951] AC 737

- Aircraft: *Fosbroke-Hobbes* v. *Airwork Ltd* [1937] 1 All ER 108
- Scaffolding and ladders (moveable structures): *Wheeler* v. *Copas* [1981] 3 All ER 405.

Who is a visitor?

There are three categories of people that are considered lawful visitors, as described below.

Those with express permission

This is a relatively straightforward category although it can be complicated if the visitor behaves in a way that exceeds the extent of the permission that has been granted. The occupier has the right to limit the way in which a visitor behaves whilst on his premises and a visitor who deviates from this will be a trespasser (covered by OLA 1984) not a lawful visitor.

EXAM TIP

The distinction between lawful visitor and trespasser is an important one as it determines which statute is relevant as the basis for liability. This makes it a popular issue in problem questions. Make sure that you can distinguish between the two by identifying what permission has been granted to the visitor and making reference to specific facts that suggest that this permission has been exceeded.

- **where** was the visitor entitled to go?
- **what** was the visitor entitled to do?
- **when** was the visitor required to leave?

Remember this useful quotation: 'when you invite a person into your house to use the staircase, you do not invite him to slide down the banisters' (*The Calgarth* [1927] P 93).

Those with implied permission

This is a slightly more problematic category as it involves those who have not been prohibited from entering the premises but have not been explicitly invited and who are assumed not to be objectionable to the occupier. For example, it is accepted that a person who enters premises wishing to speak to the occupier or to make a delivery has implied permission to do so.

Implied permission is also subject to limitations which, if exceeded, render the person a trespasser but it can be more complicated to determine the boundaries of implied permission. It would be likely to include such situations as entry into parts of property that have no relation to the purpose of his visit: for example, a delivery person may have implied permission to enter the reception area but not to wander around the gardens.

If an occupier knows that his land is used by trespassers but does nothing to prevent them from entering his land, this may amount to implied permission to enter:

KEY CASE

Lowery v. *Walker* [1911] AC 10

Concerning: trespassers; implied permission

Facts

A path across the defendant's field was used as a short cut to the railway station by several people. The defendant was aware of this and objected to it but had never taken active steps to prevent its occurrence. Without warning, the defendant put a wild horse in the field which attacked the claimant.

Legal principle

It was held that the defendant's awareness of the presence of people on his land and his failure to stop or limit their actions amounted to an implied licence to enter the property.

Those with a right to enter

The law gives rights of entry to certain categories of people which render them within the definition of lawful visitor irrespective of the wishes of the occupier of the land, e.g. police officers entering under warrant.

Those who enter premises pursuant to a contract are also deemed to be entitled to entry thus are regarded as visitors.

Duty of care

KEY STATUTORY PROVISION

Occupiers' Liability Act 1957, section 2(2)

The common duty of care is . . . to take such care as in all the circumstances of the case is reasonable to see that the visitor will be reasonably safe in using the premises for the purposes for which he is invited or permitted by the occupier to be there.

REVISION TIP

The standard of care expected resembles that applied in negligence so it would be useful to review the more detailed consideration of liability for foreseeable risks that can be found in Chapters 1 and 2.

Note the following points regarding the duty of care:

■ Although there is similarity with the standard of care in negligence, there is also an important distinction as an occupier is empowered by statute to determine the boundaries of his liability. Section 2(1) OLA 1957 provides that an occupier may extend, restrict, modify or exclude his duty to visitors by agreement or otherwise.

■ As the occupier controls the extent of the permission to enter, a visitor who acts in a manner contrary to that permission becomes a trespasser (see above).

■ The duty is to ensure that the visitor is not injured whilst on the premises. This is not the same as a duty to ensure that the premises are safe so the duty may be satisfied if the occupier displays warning signs or cordons off areas that are dangerous.

■ There are situations in which the common duty of care differs, as illustrated in Figure 6.1.

Figure 6.1

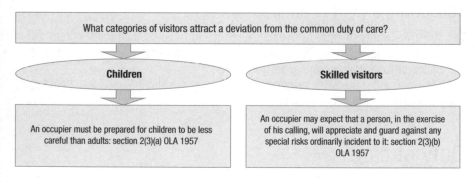

Children

Although section 2(3)(a) warns that children are less careful than adults, implying that greater care may be needed to protect them from harm, case law has sought to balance responsibility between occupiers and parents.

KEY CASE

Phipps v. *Rochester Corporation* [1955] 1 QB 450

Concerning: child visitors

Facts

A five-year-old child played on land under development by the local council. On one occasion, he fell down a trench dug by the council.

Legal principle

The court held that the defendant was entitled to assume that parents would take primary responsibility for the safety and control of their children. As a prudent parent would not have allowed a child of that age to play on a building site unattended, there was no liability as the defendant could not have been expected to protect against unforeseeable risks.

The policy behind this decision was that it was not socially desirable for parents to shift the burden of protecting their children from harm from themselves to landowners.

It is likely, however, that a duty will exist if land holds concealed dangers or allurements that tempt the children into danger:

KEY CASE

Glasgow Corporation v. *Taylor* [1922] 1 AC 44

Concerning: child visitors

Facts

A seven-year-old child died after eating poisonous berries in a public park. The plants were fenced off but there were no notices warning that the berries were poisonous.

Legal principle

It was held that the plants did not present an obvious risk of danger so the council should have taken measures to draw attention to the concealed danger that they represented. The court also commented that an occupier who is aware that something on his land would act as an allurement to children (such as berries that look edible) must take greater care to protect against this risk involved.

The level of care expected will depend upon the nature of the risk and the age and awareness of the child. For example, in *Titchener* v. *BRB* [1983] 3 All ER 770, no duty was owed to a 15-year-old boy who was struck by a train whilst walking on a railway line at night as he was aware of the dangers posed by his activity.

Skilled visitors

The law expects skilled visitors whose expertise gives them greater awareness of risks of harm than the ordinary occupier to take precautions to protect themselves. This does not mean that occupiers have no duty towards skilled visitors; it depends on the nature of the risk. See Figure 6.2.

Figure 6.2

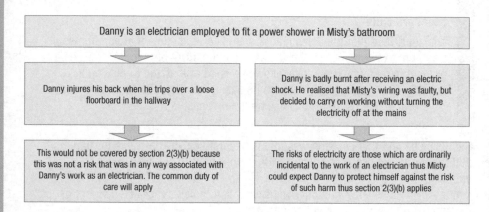

Warning signs

Occupiers' Liability Act 1957, section 2(4)(a)

Where damage is caused to a visitor by a danger of which he had been warned by the occupier, the warning is not to be treated without more as absolving the occupier from liability, unless in all the circumstances it was enough to enable the visitor to be reasonably safe.

The following factors should be taken into account when considering whether a warning sign was 'enough to enable the visitor to be reasonably safe':

▎ How specific was the warning? For example, consider the difference between 'Caution' and 'Caution: slippery surface'; the warning should be sufficiently precise so that the visitor knows what risk he is facing.

▎ How obvious was the danger? Hidden dangers necessitate greater efforts to call attention to them than readily apparent risks. In *Staples* v. *West Dorset District Council* [1995] 93 LGR 536, it was held that the risk posed by wet algae on a high wall were so obvious that there was no need for a warning sign.

- Is the sign combined with other safety measures? The use of fencing or barriers emphasises the need for safety.
- What sort of visitor is targeted? Something more than a sign may be needed to guard against risks that are linked to children.

FURTHER THINKING

An occupier may try to avoid liability by using an exclusion notice rather than a warning sign. A detailed consideration of exclusion clauses is beyond the scope of this book, being an issue covered in the law of contract. However, the following is an accessible and interesting article on exclusion clauses and occupiers' liability that would be useful reading to refresh your memory:

Mesher, J., 'Occupiers, Trespassers and the Unfair Contract Terms Act 1977' (1979) *Conveyancer* 58

Liability for independent contractors

Section 2 (4)(b) OLA 1957 specifies three circumstances in which an occupier is liable for harm caused to a visitor by the work of an independent contractor:

- If it was unreasonable to entrust the work to an independent contractor, i.e. if it was work that the occupier could, in the circumstances, have carried out himself
- If the occupier failed to take reasonable steps to ensure that the contractor was competent
- If the occupier failed to take reasonable care to ensure that the work was carried out to an appropriate standard.

EXAM TIP

If you encounter issues relating to an independent contractor in a problem question, consider the following:

What did the occupier do to check the competence of the contractor?

- Did he take up references?
- Did he check that the contractor was qualified or registered with a trade association?
- Did he ask to see examples of his work?

What did the occupier do to check the quality of the work?

- Did he make periodic inspections when the work was in progress?
- Did he ask for progress reports?
- Did he inspect the finished work?

The occupier is only expected to do what is reasonable to check the quality of the work and this will vary according to the complexity and technical intricacy of the work. See Figure 6.3.

Figure 6.3

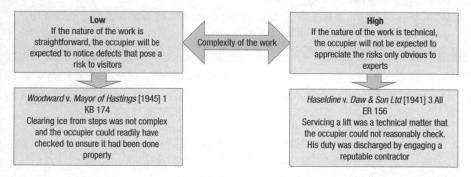

Defences

The following are ways in which an occupier could seek to limit or avoid liability:

■ *Volenti non fit injuria*: this asserts that the visitor consented to the risk of injury as he knew of and understood and accepted the risk of injury: section 2(5) OLA 1957
■ Reliance on exclusion or limitation of liability by the use of notices (see above)
■ Contributory negligence: under the Law Reform (Contributory Negligence) Act 1945, damages awarded to the claimant will be reduced to the extent that the court accepts that he is responsible for his own injuries or loss.

REVISION NOTE

Contributory negligence and *volenti non fit injuria* (consent) are general defences which are available to most torts in addition to occupiers' liability. You will find a more detailed outline of the elements of these defences and their operation in Chapter 11. You may find it useful to take a look at these defences and consider how they would operate in relation to occupiers' liability.

■Occupiers' Liability Act 1984

OLA 1984 extended the protection of the law to cover:

■ Trespassers
■ People lawfully exercising private rights of way
■ Visitors to land covered by section 60 of the National Parks and Access to the Countryside Act 1949 and 'right to room' legislation.

The scope of the protection is narrower than OLA 1957 in relation to lawful visitors as, according to section 1(1) OLA 1984, an occupier may be liable for injuries only and not damage to property. Other than this and its application to trespassers, the provisions of OLA 1984 mirror OLA 1957.

Who is a trespasser?

There is no statutory definition but case law has formulated a definition which has been generally accepted. Do not be concerned that the definition pre-dates the relevant legislation; this often happens when the common law has defined a term in a way that needs no amendment.

A **trespasser** is 'someone who goes on the land without invitation of any sort and whose presence is either unknown to the proprietor or, if known, is practically objected to': *Robert Addie & Sons (Collieries) Ltd* v. *Dumbreck* [1929] AC 358.

Duty of care

Section 1(3) OLA 1984 outlines three conditions that must be satisfied for a duty to arise:

■ The occupier must be aware of the danger or have reasonable grounds to believe that it exists (subjective);
■ He knows or has reasonable grounds to believe that a trespasser is in the vicinity of the danger (subjective); and,
■ The risk is one against which, in all the circumstances, he may reasonably be expected to offer some protection (objective: based on the reasonable occupier).

The first two aspects of section 1(3) are based upon the occupier's actual knowledge of the risk and the presence of trespassers. Look for evidence of this in the facts. For example:

■ Is there evidence that the land is used as a short cut?
■ Is there a secure and undamaged boundary fence?
■ Has the occupier noticed risks on his land?
■ Is the occupier aware of previous accidents?

The third element is based upon the reasonableness of imposing liability. Factors to take into account include:

■ The nature and extent of the risk, i.e. whether it was obvious or hidden and the severity of the harm that it posed.
■ What sort of trespassers are involved? An occupier may be expected to take greater precautions to protect against harm to child trespassers than to adults.
■ Could the danger have been reduced or negated by precautions? Did any precautions taken meet the standards of the reasonable occupier?

Signs and defences

In this respect, there is no distinction with the provisions outlined in relation to OLA 1957.

▌Chapter summary:
▌Putting it all together

TEST YOURSELF

☐ Can you tick all the points from the revision checklist at the beginning of this chapter?

☐ Take the **end-of-chapter quiz** on the companion website.

☐ Test your knowledge of the cases with the **revision flashcards** on the website.

☐ Attempt the problem question from the beginning of the chapter using the guidelines below.

☐ Go to the companion website to try out other questions.

Answer guidelines

See the problem question at the start of the chapter. A diagram illustrating how to structure your answer is available on the website.

1 Follow the instructions in the question. You are asked to advise Omar so make sure that this is what you do rather than engaging in a discussion from the perspective of the claimants.
2 Remember that the relevant statute is determined by the status of the person injured so give close consideration to whether each of the parties is a lawful visitor or trespasser.
3 Take each potential claimant separately, using headings if you feel that this will add clarity to your answer, and work through the requirements for liability. Establish issues common to all three parties (such as occupier and premises) in relation to the first claimant and avoid repetition by referring back to your previous discussion with clear signposting. For example, 'Omar is the occupier of these premises, as discussed earlier' or 'Lucy satisfies the requirements of a lawful visitor as outlined above as she has permission to enter the premises as part of her employment'.
4 Warning signs feature in relation to two of the parties so be sure to give this issue detailed attention. Reference to the questions outlined in this chapter should help you to determine whether or not sufficient warning has been given to Lew and Maggie.

Make your answer really stand out

▪ Do not forget to discuss the role of the independent contractor. As your role is to advise Omar, he will be particularly interested in any ways that he can avoid liability, but remember that your answer must be an objective evaluation that looks at both sides of the argument rather than being slanted towards what the client wants to hear.

▪ Do give adequate discussion to the question of whether Lew is a lawful visitor or a trespasser. There are plenty of factors that can be taken into account raised by the question so be sure to make use of specific facts when determining this issue. In particular, when considering Omar's liability to Lew, do not overlook his age and the absence of his mother.

7
Nuisance

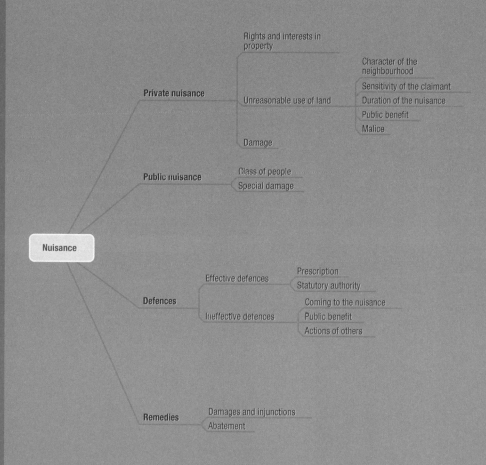

Nuisance

- Private nuisance
  - Rights and interests in property
  - Unreasonable use of land
    - Character of the neighbourhood
    - Sensitivity of the claimant
    - Duration of the nuisance
    - Public benefit
    - Malice
  - Damage

- Public nuisance
  - Class of people
  - Special damage

- Defences
  - Effective defences
    - Prescription
    - Statutory authority
  - Ineffective defences
    - Coming to the nuisance
    - Public benefit
    - Actions of others

- Remedies
  - Damages and injunctions
  - Abatement

Revision checklist

What you need to know:

☐ The elements of private nuisance and its role in protecting rights in land including key concepts concerning the unreasonable use of land such as malice, the sensitivity of the claimant and the character of the neighbourhood

☐ The role of public nuisance and the relevance of key concepts such as the class of people affected and the requirement for special damage

☐ The distinction between private and public nuisance and their relationship with other property torts such as trespass to land

☐ The nature and operation of defences and the availability of remedies.

Introduction:
Nuisance

Nuisance may be private (affecting a particular individual or property) or public (impacting on a wider group of people).

Private nuisance is concerned with the protection of proprietary rights and interests hence its essence is to uphold the right to quiet enjoyment of one's own land. By contrast, it is a requirement of public nuisance that a section of the public is affected and it lacks any requirement for a nexus between the nuisance and property. Both torts raise issues of environmental protection as they cover topics such as noise and pollution but this is just a side effect of the scope of nuisance; remember that it is a tort aimed at protecting individuals not the environment generally.

Nuisance is one of the key ways in which individuals can secure a peaceful existence free from external interference. Given the premium placed on freedom from aggravation in today's society, nuisance has a key role to play in upholding an individual's interest in a quiet life. This is a very popular examination topic thus should play a central role in your revision strategy.

Essay question advice

Essays on nuisance are relatively common. They may deal with private or public nuisance or a combination of the two, in which case an awareness of the relationship between them and any overlap is necessary. An essay could take a broader focus on the way in which tort protects property rights, in which case an ability to comment on nuisance and other torts such as negligence and trespass to land is essential.

Problem question advice

Nuisance is a common topic for problem questions. Again, private and public nuisance may combine to test the student's ability to differentiate between the two torts. The same applies to trespass to land (mutually exclusive with private nuisance) and negligence so it could be beneficial to regards these torts as a useful group of revision topics.

Sample question

Could you answer this question? Below is a typical problem question that could arise on this topic. Guidelines on answering the question are included at the end of the chapter, whilst a sample essay question and guidance on tackling it can be found on the companion website.

Problem question

Harry owns a house, from which he also runs his own business, that adjoins a field in which donkeys are kept. Recently, the owners of the field have increased the number of donkeys kept there and have commenced construction of a large barn and stables. The noise from the construction disturbs Harry during the day as his office overlooks the construction and the braying of the donkeys disturbs his sleep. Other people in the neighbourhood have also complained about the noise of the donkeys and the building works. During the construction, the large crane used to move building materials into the field dropped a pallet of bricks, sending debris into Harry's garden and injuring his gardener, Nim, who was working in the garden at the time. Harry is also aggrieved because the trees in the field are increasingly overhanging his driveway, making it difficult for him to park his car without scratching the paintwork.

Discuss the liability for nuisance arising from this situation.

■Private nuisance

KEY DEFINITION

'The very essence of **private nuisance** . . . is the unreasonable use of man of his land to the detriment of his neighbour': *Miller* v. *Jackson* [1977] 3 All ER 338

The definition makes it clear that private nuisance focuses around interference with land or property that stems from neighbouring land or property. This can take several forms, as illustrated in Figure 7.1.

Figure 7.1

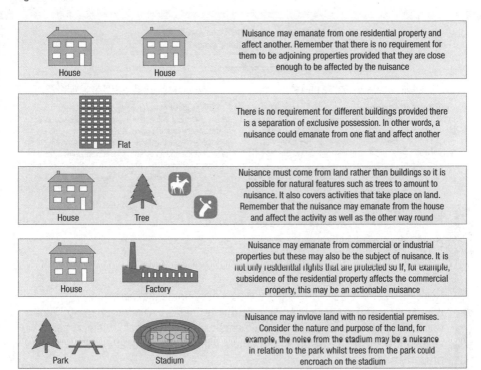

House House	Nuisance may emanate from one residential property and affect another. Remember that there is no requirement for them to be adjoining properties provided that they are close enough to be affected by the nuisance
Flat	There is no requirement for different buildings provided there is a separation of exclusive possession. In other words, a nuisance could emanate from one flat and affect another
House Tree	Nuisance must come from land rather than buildings so it is possible for natural features such as trees to amount to nuisance. It also covers activities that take place on land. Remember that the nuisance may emanate from the house and affect the activity as well as the other way round
House Factory	Nuisance may emanate from commercial or industrial properties but these may also be the subject of nuisance. It is not only residential rights that are protected so If, for example, subsidence of the residential property affects the commercial property, this may be an actionable nuisance
Park Stadium	Nuisance may invlove land with no residential premises. Consider the nature and purpose of the land, for example, the noise from the stadium may be a nuisance in relation to the park whilst trees from the park could encroach on the stadium

This emphasises that the two central characteristics of private nuisance are

▮ Protection of land or property
▮ From unreasonable interference.

Rights and interests in property

As private nuisance is concerned to protect interests in and enjoyment of land, it was considered fundamental that a person could only enjoy the protection of this tort if they had the right to exclusive possession of the land, e.g. the owner or leaseholder. This placed limitations on the availability of an action in private nuisance as visitors, lodgers and family members were not entitled to claim so the principle became challenged in the courts. See Figure 7.2.

Figure 7.2

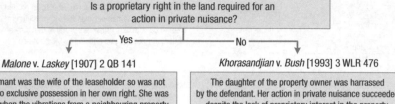

Is a proprietary right in the land required for an action in private nuisance?

Yes — *Malone* v. *Laskey* [1907] 2 QB 141

The claimant was the wife of the leaseholder so was not entitled to exclusive possession in her own right. She was injured when the vibrations from a neighbouring property caused a toilet cistern to fall on her head. Her claim was rejected as she lacked a proprietary interest in the land

No — *Khorasandjian* v. *Bush* [1993] 3 WLR 476

The daughter of the property owner was harrassed by the defendant. Her action in private nuisance succeeded despite the lack of proprietary interest in the property, probably because there was no clear need for an injunction to protect her and no other basis upon which this could be issued (as the case occurred prior to the Protection from Harassment Act 1997: see Chapter 9)

KEY CASE

Hunter v. *Canary Wharf* [1997] 2 All ER 426

Concerning: interest in land

Facts

Residents in the area of the Canary Wharf development experienced interference with the television signals due to the construction of an 800 foot metal-plated tower. Some of the claimants were homeowners whilst others were family members, lodgers and others without a proprietary interest in the property affected.

Legal principle

The Court of Appeal had ruled that occupation of a home was a sufficient basis for a claim but this was reversed by the House of Lords who reinstated the requirement of a proprietary interest stated in *Malone* v. *Laskey* (with the amendment that a wife's beneficial interest in the family home conferred a proprietary right upon her).

This decision restated private nuisance as a tort concerned with property rights and not one which protected against nuisance caused to individuals independently as it can only be brought by a person with rights to exclusive possession of the property such as an owner or tenant (or non-resident landlord if the nuisance is likely to cause permanent damage to his property).

Unreasonable use of land

It is essential to identify what situations fall within unreasonable use of land. However, reasonableness is not an absolute concept and consideration of the following factors will help to determine whether or not a particular use of land is reasonable:

- Character of the neighbourhood
- Sensitivity of the claimant
- Duration of the nuisance
- Public benefit
- Malice of the defendant.

Character of the neighbourhood

What is reasonable depends upon the location in which it takes place. It might be reasonable to operate a steelworks in an industrial area but not in the midst of a housing development.

The character of the neighbourhood is only a consideration if the nuisance complained of concerns inconvenience to the claimant, e.g. loss of sleep, or loss of enjoyment of property, e.g. smells that make it unpleasant to sit in the garden. If the nuisance causes physical damage, the character of the neighbourhood is irrelevant: *St Helen's Smelting Co* v. *Tippings* (1865) 11 HL Cas 642 (where acid smuts from the smelting works damaged trees and plants on the claimant's land).

EXAM TIP

Remember that whether something amounts to a nuisance will depend on a range of factors including the location where it takes place. Examiners may test this knowledge by including an example of a nuisance from case law but varying the nature of the area in which it takes place.

The key point to note here is that 'what would be a nuisance in Belgrave Square would not necessarily be so in Bermondsey' (*Sturges* v. *Bridgeman* (1879) 11 Ch D 852). Demonstrate understanding by reformulating this principle in contemporary terms: e.g. the noise from factories may be tolerated in a heavily industrial area but not in the countryside.

Sensitivity of the claimant

The existence of nuisance is determined by considering its effect on a reasonable person and ordinary land use. If the claimant was unusually sensitive or was using his own land for an unusual purpose that made it particularly sensitive to disruption, he will not be able to rely on nuisance unless the action complained of would have disturbed a reasonable person.

Robinson v. _Kilvert_ (1889) 41 Ch D 88

Concerning: sensitivity of the claimant

Facts

The claimant carried out a trade involving heat-sensitive paper. He sought to bring an action in private nuisance against the occupier of the cellar in the same building as the heat from the defendant's trade damaged his paper.

Legal principle

It was held that the reasonable use of land would not become unreasonable merely because it affected someone with a particular sensitivity unless 'it interferes with the ordinary enjoyment of life, or the ordinary use of property for the purposes of residence or business'.

Figure 7.3 demonstrates the questions that need to be addressed to determine whether the claimant fails for unusual sensitivity.

Figure 7.3

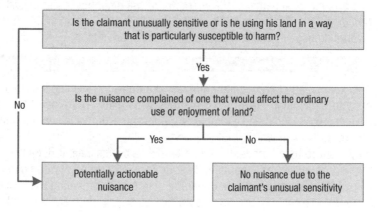

Duration of the nuisance

To be actionable, a nuisance must be continuous. This does not mean that it has to occur all the time without interruption, merely that there must be some continuity to the disturbance; for example, noise from building works every night or smell from a weekly market.

Public benefit

The greater the general utility of the defendant's actions, the less likely it is that it will amount to an actionable nuisance. For example, building works that benefit the community may disturb residents in the immediate vicinity but the public benefit of the work will outweigh the inconvenience to individuals unless other factors make the nuisance unreasonable, such as a failure to take reasonable measures to minimise the interruption to others.

Malice

This is one of the rare occasions in law where malice on the part of the defendant contributes to liability. If the defendant acts out of hostility or spite, his actions are likely to fall within private nuisance even though they would not otherwise amount to an unreasonable use of land. It has been held that it is not 'a legitimate use of the defendant's house to use it for the purpose of vexing and annoying his neighbour' (*Christie* v. *Davey* [1893] 1 Ch 316: the defendant banged metal trays and hammered on the wall to disrupt music lessons given by his neighbour).

KEY CASE

Hollywood Silver Fox Farm Ltd v. *Emmett* [1936] 2 KB 468

Concerning: malicious interruption

Facts

The defendant persistently fired his shotgun on his own land in order to disrupt the breeding of foxes on a neighbouring farm as he felt that the fur farm devalued his own land which he was trying to sell.

Legal principle

Whilst it was not unreasonable for a farmer to fire a shotgun on his own land, the fact that the defendant did so with the aim of disrupting the lawful activities of his neighbour changed the character of his actions and rendered them unreasonable and an actionable nuisance.

EXAM TIP

Look out for evidence of ill-will or malice that motivates the defendant's actions. If there is no express motive stated, try to infer one from the surrounding facts. If the facts are ambiguous, remember to present both sides of the argument and note the difference in outcome raised by an adverse motive.

Damage

Private nuisance is not actionable *per se* thus the claimant must suffer some harm, injury or damage in order to succeed with a claim. In *Hunter* v. *Canary Wharf* [1997] 2 All ER 426, Lord Lloyd identified three categories of damage that give rise to an actionable private nuisance; see Figure 7.4.

Figure 7.4

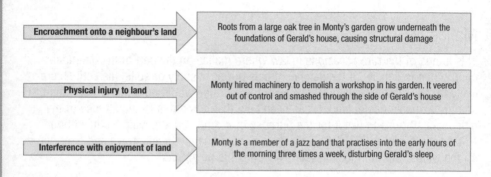

| Encroachment onto a neighbour's land | Roots from a large oak tree in Monty's garden grow underneath the foundations of Gerald's house, causing structural damage |

| Physical injury to land | Monty hired machinery to demolish a workshop in his garden. It veered out of control and smashed through the side of Gerald's house |

| Interference with enjoyment of land | Monty is a member of a jazz band that practises into the early hours of the morning three times a week, disturbing Gerald's sleep |

■Public nuisance

KEY DEFINITION

Public nuisance 'materially affects the reasonable comfort and convenience of life of a class of Her Majesty's subjects' (*A-G* v. *PYA Quarries Ltd* [1957] 2 QB 169 *per* Romer LJ).

There are two requirements that must be satisfied:

■ The nuisance has affected a class of people
■ The claimant has suffered special damage.

Class of people

There is a fair level of overlap between the sorts of conduct that may be actionable as private and public nuisance. The distinction between the torts is based upon the effect of the nuisance, not the nature of the nuisance itself. See Figure 7.5.

It is because a class of people is affected that public nuisance overlaps in terms of civil and criminal activity hence many actions are initiated by the Attorney-General. This element of injury and/or disturbance to a group is the key feature that characterises public nuisance.

Figure 7.5

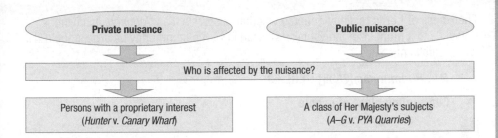

Attorney-General v. *PYA Quarries* [1957] 2 QB 169

Concerning: class of people

Facts

The process of quarrying was disrupting the local community both in terms of the dust and vibrations caused and also the scattering of splinters of rock and stone around the neighbourhood.

Legal principle

The argument that the nuisance only affected some local people and so lacked a sufficiently public nature was rejected. Lord Denning stated that a public nuisance was one which was so

widespread in range or so indiscriminate in its effect that it would not be reasonable to expect one person to take proceedings ... to put a stop to it but that it should be taken on the responsibility of the community at large.

Romer J. stated that whether or not sufficient people were affected by a nuisance for it to be said to affect a class of people was a question of fact. This has included:

- Local communities: e.g. the organisation of an 'acid house party' in a field which disturbed local residents (*R* v. *Ruffell* (1991) 13 Cr App R (S) 204)
- Groups of individuals with a particular interest: e.g. the thousands of spectators at a football match whose enjoyment was impaired by the disablement of the floodlights (*R* v. *Ong* [2001] 1 Cr App R (S) 404)
- Users of a public highway: e.g. all drivers potentially endangered by flying golf balls (*Castle* v. *St Augustine's Links* (1922) 38 TLR 615)
- Small groups of people with common characteristics: e.g. 13 female recipients of obscene telephone calls within a particular region of the country (*R* v. *Johnson* [1997] 1 WLR 367)
- Indirect impact on the community: e.g. hoax calls to the emergency services which

diverted public services away from those with genuine need (*R* v. *Lowrie* [2005] 1 Cr App R 530).

The House of Lords recently doubted whether cases such as *Johnson*, involving nuisance to a number of individuals rather than to the community at large, should fall within public nuisance.

KEY CASE

R v. *Rimmington* [2005] UKHL 63

Concerning: class of people

Facts

The defendant sent racially abusive letters to 538 people.

Legal principle

The House of Lords accepted the defendant's argument that public nuisance should not be used for conduct which is also covered by a statutory offence unless there was good reason for doing so (in this case, the conduct would have fallen within section 1 of the Malicious Communications Act 1988). Moreover, public nuisance should not be used as a means to deal with conduct that was directed at several individuals rather than at the community more generally.

FURTHER THINKING

Rimmington is an important case that has immense implications for the operation of public nuisance. A detailed analysis of its implications can be found in the following article which would make useful reading as it is always important to demonstrate up-to-date legal knowledge to your examiners:

Goldberg, J. and Grant, G., 'Public Nuisance, the Orthodox Jew and the Racist' (2005) *New Law Journal* 155(7203) 1856–7

Special damage

Although public nuisance requires inconvenience to a class of people, an action can only be brought if a particular individual (or individuals) suffer damage over and above the general inconvenience caused to the class (see Figure 7.6). This requirement limits the multitude of claims that would succeed if public nuisance was actionable on the basis of interference only (just as private nuisance is limited by the requirement of a proprietary interest).

The following kinds of damage fall within the scope of public nuisance:

I Personal injury, discomfort or inconvenience
I Damage to property
I Economic loss.

Figure 7.6

Road safety campaigners take direct action to slow down motorists on a dangerous stretch of road by digging a trench across it in the night. Can motorists Pollyanne and Tracey bring an action in public nuisance?	
Pollyanne cannot get past the trench and has to take a detour to work, arriving 30 minutes late and getting into trouble with her employer	Tracey attempts to edge her small car around the end of the trench but the edge crumbles and her car is damaged
No public nuisance Pollyanne suffers the same harm (delays in her journey) as all other members of the class affected by the nuisance (road users)	**Actionable public nuisance** Tracey has suffered additional damage over and above the delays suffered by the other members of the affected class

REVISION NOTE

Damages that fall within public nuisance must still satisfy the requirement of reasonable foreseeability outlined in *Overseas Tankship (UK) Ltd* v. *Morts Dock and Engineering Co Ltd* (*The Wagon Mound*), which is covered in detail in Chapter 2.

■ Defences

In addition to the general defences outlined in Chapter 11, the following defences are applicable to both public and private nuisance except prescription which is applicable to private nuisance only:

■ Effective defences: prescription, statutory authority
■ Ineffective defences: coming to the nuisance, public benefit, acts of others.

Effective defences

These are defences which are available and which allow the defendant to escape liability for the nuisance completely.

Prescription

A defence of prescription is effectively a claim that the defendant has acquired the right to act in a way that constitutes a private nuisance because he has done so for 20 years without interruption.

Sturges v. *Bridgeman* (1879) 11 Ch D 852

Concerning: prescriptive right

Facts

The defendant had been carrying on a confectionery business that involved the use of noisy equipment that created strong vibrations for more than 20 years. The doctor who owned the adjacent house was unable to use his newly-built consulting room because of the noise and vibration.

Legal principle

This was an actionable nuisance that was not negated by prescription because the nuisance only started once the consulting room was built. The time period commences not from the start of the act in general but from the start of it becoming a nuisance.

EXAM TIP

The distinction in *Sturges* v. *Bridgeman* is an important one. Remember to consider how long the action has been causing a nuisance rather than how long it has been going on.

Statutory authority

If the defendant's conduct was authorised by statute, it is likely to provide a defence against claims of nuisance. Some statutes specifically state that they preclude the possibility of action for nuisance, e.g. the Civil Aviation Act 1982 provides that a claim cannot lie in nuisance or trespass in relation to aircraft flying over land.

This also covers planning permission (which is granted under delegated powers exercised by local authorities) thus authorised development will not constitute an actionable nuisance unless undertaken in an unreasonable manner: *Wheeler* v. *JJ Saunders Ltd* [1996] Ch 19.

Ineffective defences

These are frequently raised arguments that are ineffectual as defences to nuisance.

EXAM TIP

Why would we include a section on ineffective defences that can never succeed? The answer is that they are frequently argued as defences to nuisance so it is important to be aware of them in order to reject them as ineffective.

Coming to the nuisance

Unless prescription authorises the nuisance, it is no defence to argue that it has carried on for a long time without attracting complaint. This is often used in situations when the claimant has actually moved into the vicinity of a nuisance that was already well established.

Do you think that the law has struck the right balance between competing interests here? Consider the following situation: Jack has been running quad-biking events on his land for five years. His previous neighbour did not object but Charlie, who moved to the area two months ago, wants an injunction to stop the activity, claiming that the constant noise causes him anxiety. Where do you think that fairness lies? The current law would protect Charlie's right to quiet enjoyment of his house without taking into account the well-established nature of Jack's business and the fact that Charlie chose to live next door. Why do you think that the law takes this approach? One argument is that it would be unreasonable for Charlie not to purchase the house of his choice merely because Jack is already acting unreasonably next door.

Remember that a critical approach to the current law can be a real strength in essays but be sure to present a balanced and objective argument.

Public benefit

The purpose of the defendant's actions is relevant to determination of its reasonableness and certainly action that is for the public good is less likely to be considered unreasonable than an action with a limited range of beneficiaries. This does not mean that a defendant can cite public benefit as a defence to a nuisance claim.

Actions of others

A defendant cannot argue that his action in isolation would not amount to a nuisance if he has knowingly taken part in a collective nuisance, e.g. one performer at an unauthorised festival that disrupts local residents.

■ Remedies

Damages and injunctions

The principal remedies for nuisance are damages and injunctions. Damages are available to compensate a claimant for physical damage to his land and in relation to personal discomfort and inconvenience. Generally, an injunction will not be granted if damages are awarded. Given the need to balance the interests of the claimant and defendant, an injunction may reflect this by limiting the nuisance rather than prohibiting it entirely. For example, in *Kennaway* v. *Thompson* [1981] QB 88, the court granted an injunction limiting the times at which the defendant could hold watersports events.

REVISION NOTE

The main remedies for trespass to land, as with so many other torts, are damages and injunctions, covered in Chapter 12. It would be useful to take a moment to refresh your memory and consider the way that these remedies operate in relation to nuisance.

Abatement

Abatement, or self-help, involves the removal of the nuisance by the claimant. In other words, the claimant rectifies the nuisance himself. As this usually involves the entry of the claimant onto the defendant's land, it generally requires prior notification unless there is an emergency situation (or if the situation can be abated without entry onto the defendant's land). If the criteria for the defence are not satisfied, the claimant may be liable for trespass to land if he enters the defendant's property.

Chapter summary:
Putting it all together

TEST YOURSELF

☐ Can you tick all the points from the revision checklist at the beginning of this chapter?

☐ Take the **end-of-chapter quiz** on the companion website.

☐ Test your knowledge of the cases with the **revision flashcards** on the website.

☐ Attempt the problem question from the beginning of the chapter using the guidelines below.

☐ Go to the companion website to try out other questions.

Answer guidelines

See the problem question at the start of the chapter. A diagram illustrating how to structure your answer is available on the website.

1 The question stipulates a discussion of liability for nuisance so it is not appropriate to consider liability for any other torts that may have arisen in the facts.
2 Nuisance questions often raise a multitude of issues as is the case here. It is essential that you take time to untangle the issues so that you can identify all the relevant points and organise them into a structured answer.
3 Remember to take a structured approach to determining liability. Following the structure of this chapter could help, so that you consider (1) whether the claimant has sufficient proprietary or possessory interest to bring a claim; (2) the unreasonableness of the defendant's conduct; (3) any defences available to the defendant; and (4) what remedies the claimant could seek.

Make your answer really stand out

■ Do not draw the boundaries of the discussion too narrowly; consider liability for both private and public nuisance. It is a common mistake for students to focus exclusively on private nuisance so the ability to deal with both will please your examiner. Look out for any suggestion that a group of people are affected as this could constitute a 'class of Her Majesty's subjects' for the purposes of public nuisance. For a really strong answer, remember that the claimant must suffer special damage to bring a successful claim.
■ Do not overlook defences and remedies. Too many students concentrate on establishing liability without considering whether the defendant has a defence that would lead to a contrary outcome of a claim or what remedies are possible for the claimant. These points can attract additional credit, especially if combined with careful use of the facts to present a balanced argument. For example, Harry may only resort to abatement of the nuisance relating to the branches scratching his car if he gives advance notice or if there is an emergency.

8
Trespass to land

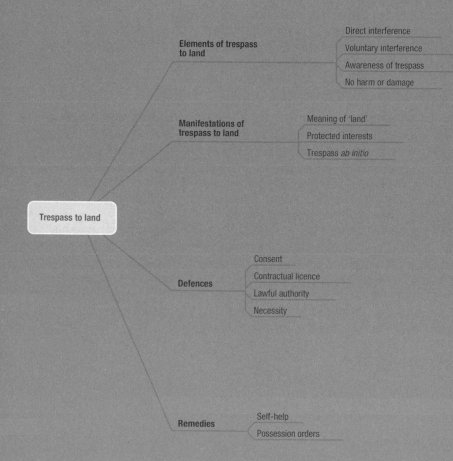

Elements of trespass to land
- Direct interference
- Voluntary interference
- Awareness of trespass
- No harm or damage

Manifestations of trespass to land
- Meaning of 'land'
- Protected interests
- Trespass *ab initio*

Trespass to land

Defences
- Consent
- Contractual licence
- Lawful authority
- Necessity

Remedies
- Self-help
- Possession orders

Revision checklist

What you need to know:

☐ The nature of trespass to land and its composite elements
☐ Definitions of key concepts such as land, possession and trespass *ab initio*
☐ The relationship between trespass to land and other torts such as nuisance
☐ The availability of defences and remedies.

Introduction:
Trespass to land

Trespass to land is a tort concerned with the prevention of interference with the possession of land.

It tends to be a misunderstood tort, possibly due to the prevalence of misleading notices stating that 'trespassers will be prosecuted' which suggest that it is a criminal offence when this is not (usually) the case. As with any tort that has a commonly understood but legally inaccurate meaning, it is important to approach the revision of this topic with a lawyer's mind to avoid reliance on inaccurate assumptions about the law.

As trespass to land is actionable *per se* (without proof of damage), it can be easy to establish. This means it may be an effective way of establishing tortious liability if other avenues fail, so plays a valuable role in tort law.

Essay question advice

Trespass to land is not a complex topic so it would be unusual for it to be the exclusive subject matter of an essay. It is likely to combine with other torts such as occupiers' liability or the other trespass torts or it could be raised in a more general question that requires examination of the extent to which tort operates to protect property rights. The level of detail given to this tort varies immensely so check your syllabus to determine how detailed your revision needs to be on this topic.

Problem question advice

There is insufficient complexity in this topic for it to form the sole subject matter of a problem question. Look for evidence of trespass to land in problem questions concerning other torts such as any suggestion of encroachment onto the land of another.

Sample question

Could you answer this question? Below is a typical problem question that could arise on this topic. Guidelines on answering the question are included at the end of the chapter, whilst a sample essay question and guidance on tackling it can be found on the companion website.

Problem question

Terry and Julie go to an art exhibition. A large notice at the entrance stated that the exhibition was open from 10am until 4pm and that smoking was strictly prohibited in the gallery. During their visit, Terry crossed into a roped off area so that Julie could take a photograph of him by his favourite picture, Waterloo Sunset. Julie did so, ignoring the sign that prohibited the use of cameras. She also took a photograph of Nelson, who was smoking a pipe. Nelson's girlfriend, Emma, was bored with the paintings and went to sleep on a secluded bench, only waking at 7pm to find the building locked and in darkness so she climbed out of an open window (which Desmond had used earlier to get into the exhibition without paying the entrance fee).

Discuss any liability for trespass to land that has arisen.

■ Elements of trespass to land

KEY DEFINITION

Trespass to land is a direct and 'unjustified interference with the possession of land ... whether or not the entrant knows that he is trespassing'. (Rogers, W.V.H. (2002) *Winfield and Jolowicz on Tort*, 16th edn, London: Sweet & Maxwell, p. 487)

Trespass to land has four elements which require further exploration:

■ There must be direct interference with the land
■ The interference must be voluntary
■ The defendant need not be aware that they are trespassing
■ There is no requirement for harm or damage.

Direct interference

As with all trespass torts, interference with the land must be direct. It is this requirement that is a key means of differentiating between trespass to land and other torts such as nuisance and negligence; see Figure 8.1.

Figure 8.1

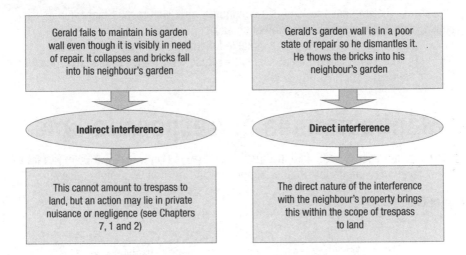

Gerald fails to maintain his garden wall even though it is visibly in need of repair. It collapses and bricks fall into his neighbour's garden

Gerald's garden wall is in a poor state of repair so he dismantles it. He thows the bricks into his neighbour's garden

Indirect interference

Direct interference

This cannot amount to trespass to land, but an action may lie in private nuisance or negligence (see Chapters 7, 1 and 2)

The direct nature of the interference with the neighbour's property brings this within the scope of trespass to land

Voluntary interference

It has long been established that a person must enter another's land voluntarily to be liable for trespass: *Smith* v. *Stone* (1647) Style 65. A person who is pushed or thrown onto land is not there voluntarily so cannot be liable but the person who pushed them there may be liable. For example, if Jack pushes Charlie into Monty's garden, it is Jack who is liable for trespass not Charlie.

Awareness of trespass

Although the entry onto the land must be voluntary, there is no requirement that the defendant is aware that he is trespassing by doing so. This gives rise to the possibility of innocent trespass if the defendant is mistaken about the ownership of land or about the availability of permission: *Conway* v. *George Wimpey & Co* [1951] 2 KB 266.

No harm or damage

Trespass to land is actionable *per se* (without any requirement for harm). This is because it is a tort which protects land against interference by allowing the owner to exclude other people and property rather than compensating for damage caused to property.

Remember that trespass to land is a continuing tort. This means that fresh liability arises as long as the tortious conduct continues. For example, if Mark places a ladder on David's land, he is liable for trespass at that point in time and will incur further liability if he subsequently refuses to remove the ladder upon David's request.

Manifestations of trespass to land

Trespass to land can be satisfied in three distinct ways (Figure 8.2). It is important to note these as they create far broader scope for the tort than you might expect.

Figure 8.2

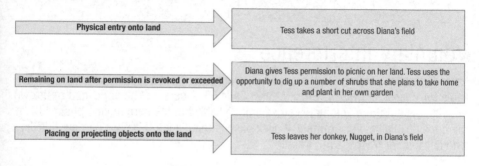

Physical entry onto land	Tess takes a short cut across Diana's field
Remaining on land after permission is revoked or exceeded	Diana gives Tess permission to picnic on her land. Tess uses the opportunity to dig up a number of shrubs that she plans to take home and plant in her own garden
Placing or projecting objects onto the land	Tess leaves her donkey, Nugget, in Diana's field

There are also three concepts that must be understood in order to appreciate the scope of trespass to land and to ensure that you recognise it when it arises:

- The meaning of 'land'
- The interest in land which is protected
- Trespass *ab initio*.

Meaning of 'land'

'Soil' and 'property' are commonly-used synonyms for 'land' but the definition adopted in relation to trespass is far broader. It includes not only the soil itself and any property built upon it as well as temporary structures and plants but also, with limits, the airspace above the land and the subsoil below the ground.

Bernstein v. Skyviews and General Ltd [1977] 2 All ER 902

Concerning: airspace; land

Facts

The defendant took aerial photographs of houses and offered them for sale to the owners. The claimant objected to this and claimed that the defendant had trespassed on his airspace in order to take the photograph.

Legal principle

It was held that the defendant had flown over the claimant's land without permission but that the right to ownership of airspace was limited to a 'height as is necessary for the ordinary use and enjoyment of land'. This did not extend to the height at which the aircraft had flown hence the action failed.

Protected interests

It is common to refer to the owner of the land in relation to trespass but the tort actually protects against interference with the possession of land, rather than ownership (although the two may frequently coincide). If there is a division in ownership and possession, i.e. landlord and tenant, the interest that is protected is the party who is entitled to exclusive possession. This was emphasised in *AG Securities* v. *Vaughan* [1988] 3 All ER 1058 where it was also highlighted that those with licences such as guests, visitors and lodgers lack exclusive possession so cannot bring an action in trespass.

Trespass *ab initio*

A person who has permission to enter land is not a trespasser. However, an initially lawful entry becomes an actionable trespass if the defendant abuses their permission to enter the land. This is trespass *ab initio* (from the beginning) as the abuse of permission negates it from the point of entry onto the land.

EXAM TIP

Trespass *ab initio* is based upon abusive behaviour by someone with permission to be on the land. Determine whether behaviour is abusive by considering whether it was consistent with express or implied permission to enter: what was it reasonable to expect that the defendant would do on the land? For example, customers have implied permission to enter to browse and make purchases but will become trespassers if they steal whilst in a shop.

■Defences

There are four main defences to trespass to land:

- **Consent**: a person who has permission to enter is not a trespasser. Ensure that the defendant has not exceeded the limits of his permission.
- **Contractual licence**: such as payment of an entry fee or purchase of tickets for a sporting event.
- **Lawful authority**: particular people may have permission to enter particular premises in particular circumstances such as court bailiffs and the police (Police and Criminal Evidence Act 1984).
- **Necessity**: this justifies trespass in emergency situations to deal with a perceived threat. It does not matter if the threat is real provided the defendant believes that it is real.

■Remedies

In addition to damages and injunction, there are two remedies of particular importance to trespass to land:

- **Self-help**: a landowner may use reasonable force to repel or expel trespassers provided that the trespasser has not obtained full possession of the land, i.e. force cannot be used to evict squatters. Self-help can also be used to remove objects placed on land, e.g. a landowner can cut branches from trees that are encroaching onto his land, although he must ensure that the property (the cut branches) is returned to the possession of its owner.
- **Possession orders**: if a trespasser has full possession of land, an order for possession must be obtained to restore the land to its rightful owner.

REVISION NOTE

The main remedies for trespass to land, as with so many other torts, are damages and injunction, covered in Chapter 12. It would be useful to take a moment to refresh your memory and consider the way that these remedies operate in relation to trespass to land.

Chapter summary:
Putting it all together

☐ Can you tick all the points from the revision checklist at the beginning of this chapter?

☐ Take the **end-of-chapter quiz** on the companion website.

☐ Test your knowledge of the cases with the **revision flashcards** on the website.

☐ Attempt the problem question from the beginning of the chapter using the guidelines below.

☐ Go to the companion website to try out other questions.

Answer guidelines

See the problem question at the start of the chapter. A diagram illustrating how to structure your answer is available on the website.

1 Remember to introduce the topic effectively by identifying trespass to land as the relevant tort, defining it and outlining its elements.

2 In questions involving multiple parties, organisation is the key to a strong answer. Deal with each party individually so that you do not blur the issues and make sure you reach a conclusion as to liability before moving on to discuss the next party.

3 It can help to focus your mind (and your answer) if you make a list of the parties and key issues at the start:

■ **Desmond**: entered through the window, lacks permission

■ **Emma**: remained after hours (extent of permission) but was it voluntary?

■ **Nelson**: smoking prohibited, potential abuse of permission

■ **Julie**: taking photographs, potential abuse of permission

■ **Terry**: goes into a restricted area, potential abuse of permission.

Make your answer really stand out

■ Trespass to land is a relatively simple topic that is readily understood, which can lead students to skim through the elements of liability or, worse still, to reach conclusions as to liability without outlining the elements of the tort. It will impress your examiner if you treat this topic in a systematic manner, working through each element of liability in the same way that you would for the more complex torts.

■ There is a clear focus on trespass *ab initio* in the question so make sure that you deal with that issue thoroughly. By linking this to the fact that trespass to land is actionable *per se*, you could make a clever point about the purpose of the tort to protect against unwanted intrusion to land rather than to guard against damage caused to land (thus drawing a comparison with other torts).

9
Trespass to the person

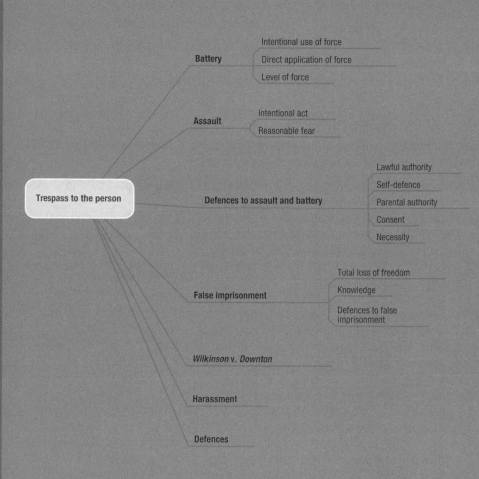

Trespass to the person

Battery
- Intentional use of force
- Direct application of force
- Level of force

Assault
- Intentional act
- Reasonable fear

Defences to assault and battery
- Lawful authority
- Self-defence
- Parental authority
- Consent
- Necessity

False imprisonment
- Total loss of freedom
- Knowledge
- Defences to false imprisonment

Wilkinson v. *Downton*

Harassment

Defences

Revision checklist

What you need to know:

- [ ] The nature of trespass to the person as a broad category
- [ ] Definitions of the individual torts that comprise trespass to the person
- [ ] The relationship between trespass to the person and other torts
- [ ] The availability and operation of defences and remedies.

Introduction:
Trespass to the person

Trespass to the person covers a collection of torts that protect the inviolability of the individual.

These torts cover a selection of ways in which an individual may suffer interference from others: physical and psychological harm, curtailment of freedom and harassment.

The ever-increasing reliance on negligence has led to trespass to the person seeming of less importance. This is unfortunate as trespass to the person, unlike negligence, is actionable *per se*, meaning that liability arises if the defendant commits the relevant act without any requirement that the claimant suffers harm. The new tort of harassment tends to be viewed as a form of trespass to the person. Although introduced to combat stalking, harassment is a broad and flexible tort that has been used in a variety of situations: domestic violence, neighbour disputes and protest situations.

These easily-established torts therefore have a useful role to play in protecting individuals against interference from others and should not be overlooked in the revision process.

Essay question advice

Essays could cover trespass to the person as a broad category or any of the individual torts that fall within it. The potential for a question on a particular tort, such as harassment, will depend upon the prominence that it has been given in your syllabus.

Essays may require a comparison between trespass to the person and other torts such as negligence or pick up on the issues raised by Articles 5, 6, 8 and 10 of the European Convention on Human Rights.

Problem question advice
Problem questions usually combine trespass with other torts to test the student's ability to identify and address a selection of torts. It is also possible that questions will require the ability to distinguish trespass to the person, which involves direct interference but requires no harm, from other torts such as negligence that differ in their requirements.

Sample question

Could you answer this question? Below is a typical essay question that could arise on this topic. Guidelines on answering the question are included at the end of the chapter, whilst a sample problem question and guidance on tackling it can be found on the companion website.

Essay question

To what extent does *Wilkinson* v. *Downton* play a useful role in protecting an individual from harm?

■Battery

KEY DEFINITION
'**Battery** is the intentional and direct application of force to another person'. (Rogers, W.V.H. (2002) *Winfield and Jolowicz on Tort*, 16th edn, London: Sweet & Maxwell, p. 71)

Battery is a straightforward tort that has the characteristics described below.

Intentional use of force

Battery requires that the defendant intentionally makes contact with the body or clothing of the claimant.

Letang v. *Cooper* [1964] 2 All ER 929

Concerning: intentional force

Facts

The defendant accidentally drove over the claimant's legs whilst she was sunbathing in a car park. She sought damages on the basis of trespass to the person as a claim in negligence was time-barred.

Legal principle

The claimant could not recover damages on the basis of trespass to the person as the defendant's actions were accidental and not intentional.

Lord Denning reiterated the mutually exclusive operation of negligence and trespass to the person:

If [the action] is intentional, it is a tort of assault and battery. If negligent and causing damage, it is the tort of negligence ... [The claimant's] only cause of action here ... (where the damage was unintentional) was negligence and not trespass to the person'.

Direct application of force

Battery requires that force is applied directly to the body of the claimant as a result of the defendant's intentional act. This requirement of directness has been interpreted broadly by the courts:

■ **Contact by a third party**. *Scott* v. *Shepherd* (1773) 2 Bl R 892: the defendant threw a lighted squib into a crowded market. It was thrown again by a third party to prevent damage to his stall, hitting the victim in the eye. The defendant was liable despite third party intervention.
■ **Contact made indirectly**. *Pursell* v. *Horn* (1838) 8 A&E 602: the defendant threw water over the claimant and was liable despite the indirect nature of the contact.
■ **Direct contact with the wrong person**. *Livingstone* v. *MoD* [1984] NI 356: a soldier fired at a rioter but missed and struck the claimant. The doctrine of transferred malice (D intends to hit A but misses and hits B) was used to establish liability for battery.

Level of force

Reference to 'force' to describe the contact required between defendant and claimant is misleading. There is no requirement that battery causes harm, indicating that the level of force may be extremely low. In *Cole* v. *Turner* (1704) 6 Mod Rep 149, it was held that 'the least touching in anger is a battery'.

The reference to anger has been interpreted to mean that the contact must be 'hostile' (*Collins* v. *Wilcox* [1984] 3 All ER 374) which has in turn been interpreted to mean that the actions were 'unlawful' (*F* v. *West Berkshire HA* [1989] 2 All ER 545) in the sense of being non-consensual.

EXAM TIP

It is a common mistake for students to conclude that there is no battery because the claimant has not suffered an injury. Remember that there is no requirement of harm caused for a battery, unlike the tort of negligence that does require that harm is caused to the claimant.

■ Assault

KEY DEFINITION

'An **assault** is an act which causes another person to apprehend the infliction of immediate, unlawful force on his person': *Collins* v. *Wilcox* [1984] 3 All ER 374 *per* Lord Goff

---

EXAM TIP

The most common error occurs when students apply the everyday meaning of 'assault' (for example, meaning 'attack') and thus confuse assault (which involves no physical contact) with battery (which does require contact).

Focus on the legal meaning of the words and concentrate on establishing the elements of the torts to avoid this problem. It can help to remember that assault usually precedes a battery.

See Figure 9.1.

Intentional act

Assault requires a deliberate act by the defendant. Although historically, 'no words or singing can amount to an assault' (*R* v. *Meade and Belt* (1823) 1 Lew CC 184), it is now clear that assault can be committed by words as well as conduct.

Figure 9.1

Timing of events →	
Assault	**Battery**

Definition	
The defendant causes the victim to apprehend immediate unlawful violence	The defendant applies non-consensual physical contact to the victim's body

In other words	
The victim sees that an attack is imminent	The attack on the victim takes place

For example	
Vincent sees Derek running towards him with an axe	Derek hits Vincent over the head with the axe

KEY CASE

R v. *Ireland* [1997] 4 All ER 225

Concerning: words as assault

Facts

The defendant made silent telephone calls to the victims. In dealing with the issue of silence as an assault, the House of Lords tackled the issue of words as an assault.

Legal principle

The proposition that 'words can never suffice [for the basis of assault] is unrealistic and indefensible. There is no reason why something said should be incapable of causing an apprehension of immediate personal violence' (*per* Lord Steyn).

Reasonable fear

The conduct must cause the claimant *reasonable fear* that attack is imminent. The reasonableness is judged according to the claimant's perceptions of the defendant's actions: *R* v. *St George* (1840) 9 C&P 483. The claimant must believe that the threatened attack is possible and will be carried out: *Thomas* v. *National Union of Mineworkers* [1985] 2 All ER 1. See Figure 9.2.

Figure 9.2

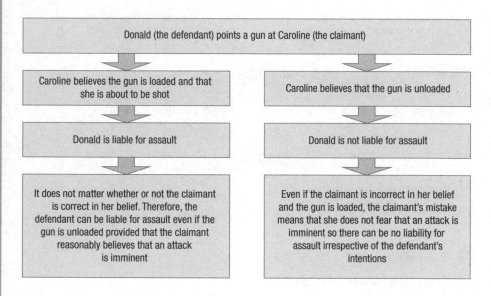

■ Defences to assault and battery

In addition to the general defences discussed in Chapter 11, there are a range of defences specific to assault and battery.

Lawful authority

Certain interferences with the person are authorised by statute such as the Police and Criminal Evidence Act 1984 which entitles the police to use reasonable force in furtherance of an arrest and the Mental Health Act 1983 which authorises the compulsory detention and treatment of those suffering from specified mental disorders.

Self-defence

A person may use such force as is reasonable to protect against an actual or perceived threat of harm against themselves or another person. The force used must be proportionate to the threat, i.e. it must be no more than is necessary to repel the threat. Force which is disproportionate will not fall within self-defence.

REVISION NOTE

Have a look at the key case of *Revill* v. *Newbury* that you will find in Chapter 11. Self-defence was not available to this householder as his actions in shooting the burglar were disproportionate to the threat posed to his property.

Parental authority

The right of a parent to use physical force to chastise a child is a hugely debated topic and one which is increasingly cited as involving human rights issues due to the possibility of contravention of Article 3 of the European Convention on Human Rights (freedom from inhumane and degrading treatment).

The use of force in punishing a child may amount to battery if the level of force is disproportionate to the child's behaviour or if the child does not understand the purpose of the punishment (*A* v. *UK* [1998] Fam LR 118).

Consent

If, for example, a person has consented to the application of force to their body a claim for battery will be defeated. Although consent is covered as a general defence in Chapter 11, it has a particular application in relation to trespass to the person. Consent may be express or implied. Consent must be given freely by a person who has the mental capacity to exercise choice and to give or withhold consent.

FURTHER THINKING

Consent in relation to trespass to the person has been particularly problematic as regards medical treatment. Many medical and surgical procedures involve bodily contact that would amount to an actionable tort of battery if the patient did not consent to the contact. This raises questions of the extent to which patients are entitled to withhold consent to necessary and often life-saving medical treatment. The issue can be complicated by questions of mental competency. The full extent of this area and the ethical issues that it raises are beyond the scope of this book but the following article provides a clear analysis of the topic that takes into account questions of human rights and would make useful reading in preparation for an essay question:

Wicks, E., 'The Right to Refuse Medical Treatment under the European Convention on Human Rights' (2001) *Medical Law Review* vol. 17, pp. 17–40

Necessity

The essence of this defence is that interference with another person may sometimes be necessary to protect them from a greater evil, e.g. grabbing someone to stop them falling over the edge of a cliff. As with consent, necessity has been used as a means of authorising medical treatment of those who are regarded as lacking the capacity to give consent, e.g. the sterilisation of a female mental patient who was involved in a sexual relationship with another patient: *Re F* [1999] 2 AC 1.

■ False imprisonment

KEY DEFINITION

False imprisonment is 'the infliction of bodily restraint which is not expressly or impliedly authorised by the law'. (Rogers, W.V.H. (2002) *Winfield and Jolowicz on Tort*, 16th edn, London: Sweet & Maxwell, p. 81)

This focuses on situations in which the claimant's liberty or movement is constrained whether this is by arrest, detention or other confinement.

REVISION NOTE

Many cases involve the arrest or detention of suspected offenders. A stronger understanding of this area can be gained by ensuring that you are familiar with the common law and statutory powers of arrest (Police and Criminal Evidence Act 1984, as amended by section 110 of the Serious Organised Crime and Police Act 2005).

Total loss of freedom

False imprisonment requires total restraint of the claimant's movements:

▌ It is not enough that the defendant cannot go where he wants provided that he can go somewhere
▌ If there is reasonable means of escape, there is no false imprisonment
▌ Restraint need not be physical. A person who is told not to leave and complies with this instruction suffers a total loss of freedom.

KEY CASE

***Bird v. Jones* (1845) 7 QB 742**

Concerning: partial constraint

Facts

The claimant partially crossed Hammersmith Bridge when it was closed during a regatta. He was prevented from continuing to the end of the bridge and claimed that this limitation on his freedom to proceed amounted to false imprisonment.

Legal principle

The claim failed because there was only partial restraint on the claimant's movement. He was not permitted to proceed but was free to retrace his steps. False imprisonment requires total, not partial, constraint on the claimant's free movement.

Knowledge

An action for false imprisonment may arise if the claimant was not aware that he was being detained at the time of the detention.

KEY CASE

***Murray v. Ministry of Defence* [1988] 2 All ER 521**

Concerning: knowledge of constraint

Facts

The claimant's house was searched in her presence and she was arrested 30 minutes later. It was unclear whether she was aware that she was not free to leave during the period prior to her arrest.

Legal principle

The House of Lords held that there was no requirement 'that the victim should be aware of the fact of denial of liberty ... [however] if a person is unaware that he has been falsely imprisoned and has suffered no harm, he can normally expect to recover no more than nominal damages' (*per* Lord Griffiths).

Defences to false imprisonment

In addition to the general defences covered in Chapter 11, the following will provide a defence to false imprisonment:

▪ **Reasonable condition for release**: if the defendant's detention of the claimant is contingent upon the performance of a reasonable condition, i.e. payment of a toll or delay based on the need to wait for appropriate transport, but the claimant refuses to comply, his continued detention will be considered voluntary;

■ **Lawful arrest**: an arrest that is made properly according to the requirements of the Police and Criminal Evidence Act 1984 (as amended) will not amount to false imprisonment nor will a detention made in furtherance of the common law right to affect a citizen's arrest;

■ **Medical detention**: there are circumstances when a person requires protection from their own behaviour and thus detention may be authorised by the provisions of the Mental Health Act 1983. Individuals suffering from particular contagious diseases may be detained against their will according to the Public Health (Control of Disease) Act 1984.

■ *Wilkinson* v. *Downton*

This case gave rise to a separate category of tortious liability based upon the infliction of indirect harm to another.

> **KEY CASE**
>
> ### *Wilkinson* v. *Downton* [1897] 2 QB 57
>
> ### Concerning: indirect harm
>
> #### Facts
>
> The defendant told the claimant that her husband had been seriously injured in an accident. This was untrue and had been meant as a practical joke. The claimant suffered a serious shock which led her to suffer adverse physical symptoms for a period of time.
>
> #### Legal principle
>
> It was held that a person who has 'wilfully done an act calculated to cause physical harm to the plaintiff – that is to say, to infringe her legal right to safety, and has in fact thereby caused physical harm to her' has provided a good cause of action (*per* Wright J).

Despite its obvious potential, particularly as it pre-dated the development of cases concerning nervous shock (see Chapter 3), this case was rarely used in this jurisdiction. The requirements for liability were clarified in a recent Court of Appeal judgment (*Wong* v. *Parkside NHS Trust* [2001] EWCA Civ 1721):

■ There must be actual harm (physical harm or recognised psychiatric illness). This differentiates this tort from other forms of trespass as they are actionable *per se*.

■ The defendant must have acted intentionally.

▮ The conduct must be of such a degree that it is calculated to cause harm so that the defendant cannot say he did not mean to cause it.

It is sometimes questioned whether the rule in *Wilkinson* v. *Downton* should fall within trespass to the person. It involves the indirect infliction of harm to an individual so satisfies the general requirement of interference with personal integrity/autonomy that characterises these torts but it does require that the claimant suffers harm which is inconsistent with the notion that trespass is actionable *per se*.

The following article would make useful reading to provide insight into the role and operation of this tort:

Lunney, M., 'Practical Joking and its Penalty: *Wilkinson* v. *Downton* in Context' (2002) *Tort Law Review* 168

▮Harassment

Prior to the enactment of the Protection from Harassment Act 1997 (PFHA), *Wilkinson* v. *Downton* was one of a variety of means used to impose tortious liability on those who caused distress and anxiety to others. The introduction of a statutory tort of harassment under section 3 PFHA obviated the need for creative use of other torts.

KEY STATUTORY PROVISION

Protection from Harassment Act 1997, section 1

Harassment is defined as the pursuit of a course of conduct that the defendant knows or ought to know amounts to harassment of another.

This breaks down into three elements, illustrated in Figure 9.3, all of which must be established for a claim of harassment to succeed.

There is no requirement that the claimant suffers physical or psychological harm as a result of the harassment. The tort is satisfied if the claimant experiences alarm or distress as a consequence of the defendant's actions, something which will vary according to the character of the victim (some people are more readily distressed than others). Once harassment is established, the claimant may obtain an injunction to prevent further harassment.

Figure 9.3

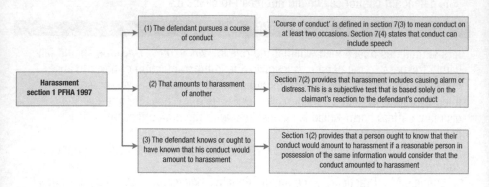

▌Defences

If the claimant establishes the elements of one of the trespass torts, the defendant may still avoid liability by reliance on a defence. Chapter 11 covers the general defences that are applicable to most torts whilst defences that are specific to particular torts involving trespass to the person have been discussed throughout this chapter.

REVISION NOTE

Make sure you are clear on which defences apply to which torts. Many students get confused on this point and lose marks as a consequence. Try making a list of each tort that details which defences are available and noting how they are likely to apply to that particular tort, i.e. consent is a general defence but the answer to the question 'consent to what?' will vary according to which tort is under consideration.

Chapter summary:
Putting it all together

☐ Can you tick all the points from the revision checklist at the beginning of this chapter?

☐ Take the **end-of-chapter quiz** on the companion website.

☐ Test your knowledge of the cases with the **revision flashcards** on the website.

☐ Attempt the essay question from the beginning of the chapter using the guidelines below.

☐ Go to the companion website to try out other questions.

Answer guidelines

See the problem question at the start of the chapter. A diagram illustrating how to structure your answer is available on the website.

1 The focus of the question indicates that you should not attempt to answer it unless you can outline the rule in *Wilkinson* v. *Downton* and comment on its operation. In particular, you should be able to explain what harm is covered by this tort.

2 Demonstrate broader understanding by situating your discussion within the context of trespass more generally. Provide a brief explanation of the scope of the other torts, noting any overlap and any gaps in coverage.

3 Avoid a common pitfall of providing excessive levels of description of the other trespass torts. Make frequent reference back to the question to ensure that your answer remains focused.

4 You should always strive to incorporate relevant case law into your answer but the use of illustrative hypothetical examples can also demonstrate understanding and support your answer. For example, can you think of a situation that is covered by *Wilkinson* v. *Downton* but not any of the other trespass torts?

Make your answer really stand out

▪ The ability to incorporate the modern restatement of the rule in *Wong* would be a useful way of illustrating up-to-date legal knowledge. It also emphasises that the tort still has a role to play in modern law.

▪ Make sure that the central point of the question is addressed by questioning whether *Wilkinson* v. *Downton* provides protection against harm that is not otherwise covered by the trespass torts. This should lead to comment about the sort of harm covered by the trespass torts. It is often noted that there is no protection from interference with an individual's privacy, for example.

▌ The ability to comment upon the role of *Wilkinson* v. *Downton* in light of the recent development of a tort of harassment and, picking up on material covered in other chapters, the evolution of liability for psychiatric injury in negligence, will demonstrate a broad range of understanding.

10
Defamation

Slander and libel

Availability of defamation

Elements of defamation
- Defamatory statement
- About the claimant
- Publication of the statement

Defences
- Privilege
- Innocent publication
- Consent
- Justification
- Fair comment
- Offer of amends

Remedies
- Damages
- Injunction

Defamation

Privacy or freedom of expression

Revision checklist

What you need to know:

- ☐ The definitions of libel and slander and the distinction between them
- ☐ The elements of defamation
- ☐ The availability and operation of the defences
- ☐ The underlying tension between an individual's right to privacy and another's right to freedom of expression.

Introduction:
Defamation

Defamation is a tort which protects a person from loss of reputation by prohibiting the publication of information likely to attract negative attention from others.

Although it is a tort which can by relied upon by any individual, many cases involve high-profile public figures in conflict with the media. This encapsulates the struggle of the law to balance between two competing rights: an individual's right to privacy (Article 8 of the European Convention on Human Rights) and the media's right to freedom of expression (Article 10). The involvement of these conflicting rights has led defamation to become more prominent as a topic for consideration since the enactment of the Human Rights Act 1998 and this establishes it as an important revision topic.

Essay question advice

Unlike many other topics, there is no real overlap between defamation and other topics in tort. This makes it a popular stand-alone essay subject. Defamation is also relatively straightforward, further increasing its popularity. The tension between privacy and freedom of expression is one of the key complexities of this topic so remember to give this particular attention during revision.

Problem question advice

Although defamation does not lend itself to combination with other torts in an essay, the same does not necessarily apply in relation to problem questions so be alert for evidence of defamatory statements in questions involving other torts. The elements of defamation are relatively straightfoward to apply but do not forget to consider whether any of the defences are raised.

Sample question

Could you answer this question? Below is a typical problem question that could arise on this topic. Guidelines on answering the question are included at the end of the chapter, whilst a sample essay question and guidance on tackling it can be found on the companion website.

Problem question

The *World of News* publishes a story about a prominent actor, Jasper Hardy, on its front page under the headline 'Pulling Power of Mr Ugly'. The story alleges that Jasper has had affairs with several married women and also a homosexual relationship. The newspaper names the first of these married women as a well-known celebrity, Gertrude Tobias, who co-presents a television show on relationship problems with her husband, Toby. The second person is described as 'drug-taking legal eagle Delores Dennis from Manchester'. This refers to a law student named Delores Dennis but many people assume it is the high-profile barrister of the same name who is based in Manchester. The final person named is Kelvin Costa who died last year from AIDS.

Consider the strengths and weaknesses of each party's claim for defamation.

■ Slander and libel

KEY DEFINITION

'**Defamation** is the publication of a[n untrue] statement which reflects on a person's reputation and tends to lower him in the estimation of right-thinking members of society generally or tends to make them shun or avoid him'. (Rogers, W.V.H. (2002) *Winfield and Jolowicz on Tort*, 16th edn, London: Sweet & Maxwell, p. 405)

Slander and libel are both forms of defamation that differ in two ways:

■ The manner in which the statement is publicised
■ The consequences that are required before damages are paid.

See Figure 10.1.

In relation to slander, there are four exceptions to the requirement for special damage to be shown. Slander is actionable *per se* if the imputation is that the claimant:

■ Has committed a serious criminal offence;
■ Is unchaste or has committed adultery (female claimants only);
■ Has a contagious or infectious disease that prevents others from associating with him; or
■ Is unfit, dishonest or incompetent in relation to his trade, profession or business.

Figure 10.1

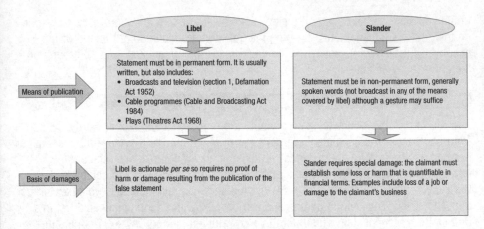

Availability of defamation

The following points should be noted:

- The dead cannot bring or defend an action for defamation; both parties must be alive.
- There is a right to trial by jury if the case is not too complex: section 69, Supreme Court Act 1981. This may be waived if both parties agree.
- Claims must be brought within 12 months: section 4A Limitation Act 1980.
- There is no public funding for defamation hence the tort favours those who can afford to protect their reputations.
- Defamation involves an unusual two-stage process. The judge determines whether the facts are capable of amounting to defamation whilst the jury decides whether the facts actually do defame the claimant.

Elements of defamation

See Figure 10.2.

Figure 10.2

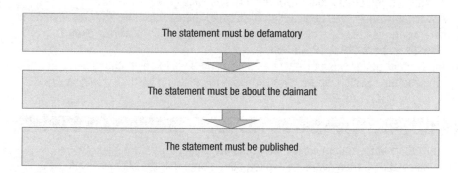

Defamatory statement

A **defamatory statement** is one that is 'calculated to injure the reputation of another, by exposing them to hatred, contempt or ridicule' (*Parmiter* v. *Coupland* (1840) 6 M&W 105) and which tends to 'lower the [claimant] in the estimation of right-thinking members of society' (*Sim* v. *Stretch* (1936) 52 TLR 669).

What sort of allegation lowers a person in the eyes of right-thinking members of society?

KEY CASE

***Byrne* v. *Deane* [1937] 2 All ER 204**

Concerning: reputation; right-thinking persons

Facts

The claimant was a member of a golf club who was vilified in verse for reporting the presence of a popular but illegal gaming machine in the clubhouse.

Legal principle

Anyone who would think less of a person for reporting illegal activity to the police was not a right-thinking member of society so the words could not be defamatory on that basis. (The case succeeded as the verse also implied disloyalty to his club, something that would erode his standing in the eyes of right-thinking members of society.)

The following have amounted to defamatory statements:

▪ An actor was described as hideously ugly: *Berkoff* v. *Birchill* [1996] 4 All ER 1008

- An actor was said to be homosexual and deliberately suppressing this to preserve an image of heterosexuality: *Donovan* v. *The Face* (1992, unreported)
- A married woman was depicted as unmarried thus suggesting she was 'living in sin' (a serious social problem at the time): *Cassidy* v. *Daily Mirror Group Newspapers Ltd* [1929] 2 KB 331
- An amateur golfer was portrayed as endorsing a well-known chocolate manufacturer (which would have removed his amateur status): *Tolley* v. *Fry & Sons Ltd* [1931] AC 331.

EXAM TIP

Remember that a statement can be impliedly defamatory. In the last two examples above, there were no explicit statements that the claimant was unmarried or sponsored by a chocolate manufacturer. Liability arose from pictures and their accompanying captions: in the first case describing the wife as a fiancée whilst the second was an advertisement that implied that the claimant endorsed the product.

If a statement is not explicitly defamatory, take note of the meaning that the right-thinking person would take from the publication as a whole.

About the claimant

The claimant must establish that the defamation refers to him. This is usually obvious if he is named or otherwise identified in the statement.

A claimant may also have an action if a statement does not refer to him but there are grounds upon which others might think that it did:

KEY CASE

Newstead v. *London Express Newpaper Ltd* [1940] 1 KB 377

Concerning: mis-identification of claimant

Facts

The defendant newspaper reported that Harold Newstead, aged 30 of Camberwell, was convicted of bigamy. Although this was true, another Harold Newstead from Camberwell of that age brought an action for libel on the basis that it was untrue (and defamatory) in relation to him.

Legal principle

It was held that the statement was defamatory as the reasonable person would think that the statement referred to the claimant.

- The claimant need not be named provided there is sufficient information from which he can be identified, even wrongly, with the statement: *Morgan* v. *Odhams*

Press [1971] 1 WLR 1239. It is irrelevant that the publisher intended to refer to someone else other than the claimant and did not know that the claimant existed or that others would think that the statement referred to him.

■ A statement which is defamatory to a broad class of persons, e.g. university lecturers cannot be relied upon by individuals within that class unless they are specifically identified. Only if the class is defined sufficiently narrowly, e.g. lecturers in a particular subject at a specific university, so that it could be seen as referring to them as individuals, can it form the basis of defamation: *Knuppfer* v. *London Express Newspapers* [1944] 1 All ER 495.

Publication of the statement

It is usual to think of publication of defamatory statements to the world in general via the media but defamation only requires that one other person must hear or read the statement. The publication requirement reinforces the purpose of defamation, which is to protect the reputation of the individual, not his feelings; a statement made exclusively to the claimant cannot damage his reputation in the eyes of others so cannot be defamatory.

■ Defences

There are a range of defences that may defeat a claim for defamation even if the claimant has established the elements of the tort.

Privilege

This refers to circumstances in which it is regarded as imperative that people are able to express their views without fear of legal action. As such, it represents the primacy of the interests of freedom of expression over the rights of the individual in protecting his reputation. See Figure 10.3.

Innocent publication

It is not defamation for a person, who is not the author, editor or publisher of the material, to reproduce material that they did not believe contained defamatory comment provided that they took reasonable care in publishing the statement: section 1, Defamation Act 1996.

Figure 10.3

Absolute privilege
Covers: statements made during judicial and parliamentary proceedings where there is an interest in ensuring that parties are able to speak their minds without fear of legal proceedings
Effect: cannot be relied upon in legal proceedings under any circumstances

Qualified privilege
Covers: situations in which there is a moral or legal duty to disclose information even if it is unfavourable to the claimant such as an employment reference
Effect: can only be relied upon if the defendant acted with malice in making the defamatory statement

Consent

A person who consents to publication cannot subsequently bring an action for defamation.

Justification

A statement which is true in relation to the claimant cannot be defamatory so the defendant may rely on the defence of justification if he is able to establish the accuracy of the statement. The law requires only that he establishes that the central defamatory thrust of the statement is true; justification will still provide a defence if there are peripheral inaccuracies in the statement: section 5, Defamation Act 1952.

Fair comment

This defence applies to critical comment based upon true facts. It generally involves media comments about matters of public interest and the defence regards that the person making the comment must believe it to be based in truth and must not be acting maliciously. It is, in effect, opinion based upon true statements.

In relation to whether the comment is fair, it has been said that 'the true test is whether the opinion, however exaggerated, obstinate or prejudiced, was honestly held by the person expressing it': *Reynolds* v. *Times Newspapers* [2001] 2 AC 127. This approach to the fairness of the comment is regarded as important in protection of freedom of expression: *Silkin* v. *Beaverbrook Newspapers* [1958] 1 WLR 743.

Offer of amends

This is not a defence, strictly speaking, as it allows a defendant to pre-empt legal proceedings.

KEY STATUTORY PROVISION

Defamation Act 1996, section 2

Provides that the publisher of a defamatory statement may make amends and thus avoid liability if he:

▮ Makes a suitable correction and apology
▮ Publishes these in a reasonable manner
▮ Pays compensation to the claimant.

▮Remedies

Remedies in tort are discussed in more detail in Chapter 12. The following outlines the points that are particularly pertinent to defamation.

Damages

The primary remedy for a successful claimant is damages which, unusually, are determined by the jury following the issue of guidelines by the judge about the likely impact of their decision: *Sutcliffe* v. *Pressdram* [1991] 1 QB 153. The Courts and Legal Services Act 1990 provides that the quantum of damages can be reassessed by the Court of Appeal if the award by the jury is inappropriate, such as the reduction from £250,000 to £110,000 in *Rantzen* v. *Mirror Group Newspapers* [1994] QB 670.

Whilst the general aim of an award of damages is to compensate the claimant for loss suffered as a result of the defendant's tortious behaviour, the law acknowledges the difficulties of quantification of the loss involved in defamation by allowing the award of exemplary damages to take account of both the loss of reputation and the 'distress, hurt and humiliation' caused by the publication: *John* v. *Mirror Group Newspapers* [1996] 2 All ER 35.

Injunction

There are two roles for injunction in defamation cases:

▮ An interlocutory injunction can be obtained to prevent publication of defamatory material if the claimant is aware that this is likely

■ An injunction can be sought after a successful defamation claim if the claimant can establish that there is a real risk of repetition of the publication.

■Privacy or freedom of expression

Defamation focuses attention on the debate about the appropriate balance between an individual's right to privacy and the conflicting right to freedom of expression.

KEY CASE

***A* v. *B plc* [2002] 2 All ER 504**
Concerning: privacy; freedom of expression

Facts

A professional footballer sought to prevent publication of 'kiss and tell' revelations on the basis that they interfered with his right to a private life.

Legal principle

It was held that scurrilous stories of casual sexual encounters deserved little protection so the right of the other party involved and the newspaper to freedom of expression should prevail. The Court of Appeal was clear that the newspapers should be free to publish without constraint provided they were within the Press Complaints Commission Code.

The story in this case was true so the claimant could not rely on defamation to prevent publication; the case merely demonstrates the tension between privacy and freedom of expression.

FURTHER THINKING

Defamation cannot protect individuals who wish to suppress the publication of unfavourable or sensitive information if it is true. This makes defamation of only limited value in protecting an individual's reputation as it is limited in scope to untrue statements. The role of defamation in modern society and its role in the balance between rights to privacy and freedom of expression are outlined with clarity in the following article, which would be valuable reading in preparation for an essay question:

Squires, D.B., 'Striking the Balance between Kissers and Tellers: the Law of Breach of Confidence' (1999) *Entertainment Law Review* vol. 10, pp. 240–243

Chapter summary:
Putting it all together

☐ Can you tick all the points from the revision checklist at the beginning of this chapter?

☐ Take the **end-of-chapter quiz** on the companion website.

☐ Test your knowledge of the cases with the **revision flashcards** on the website.

☐ Attempt the problem question from the beginning of the chapter using the guidelines below.

☐ Go to the companion website to try out other questions.

Answer guidelines

See the problem question at the start of the chapter. A diagram illustrating how to structure your answer is available on the website.

1 The question requires an evaluation of the claims of each of the parties so make sure that everyone with a potential claim, even if it is inevitable that it will be unsuccessful, is identified: Jasper, Gertrude, Toby, Delores (student), Delores (barrister) and Kelvin.

2 Discuss each party in turn and work through the elements of defamation to see if an action is available. Do not be tempted to combine a discussion of any of the parties to save time or words or because they seem to raise the same issues as this will result in poor structure and lack of clarity.

3 Your answer should be organised. Discuss (1) availability; (2) elements; (3) defences; and (4) remedies in relation to each party. The discussion of the elements of defamation should form the bulk of the answer and should include the three considerations identified in this chapter: (1) defamatory statement (2) about the claimant (3) that is published.

4 If you find unequivocal evidence that the claim will fail, state this and move on to discuss another party. For example, Kelvin cannot bring a claim because he is dead. This should be the extent of your discussion of his claim; there is no merit in going on to consider whether the statement amounts to defamation against him.

Make your answer really stand out

▪ Think carefully about the way in which the facts could be used. For example, Kelvin's death precludes him from bringing an action but the fact that he died from

AIDS may be useful in relation to the claims of the other parties, given the communicable nature of the disease.

■ Most students address the availability of defamation and its elements but give little or no attention to defences and remedies. Make sure that your discussion is complete by including these points.

■ The question requires a discussion of the strengths and weaknesses of the claims so make sure that you adhere to this instruction and provide a balanced evaluation of the potential claims.

11
Defences

Consent – *volenti non fit injuria*
- Knowledge of the risk
- Consent of the claimant
  - Employees
  - Passengers in vehicles
  - Participants and spectators

Illegality – *ex turpi causa non oritur actio*

Defences

Contributory negligence
- Claimant's damage
- Claimant's fault
- Standard of care
  - Children
  - Rescuers
  - Emergency situations
- Apportionment of blame

Specific defences

Revision checklist

What you need to know:

- [ ] The elements and availability of the three general defences
- [ ] The relationship between the absolute defences and the partial defence of contributory negligence
- [ ] The relevance of particular categories of claimants such as children, employees and passengers in motor vehicles
- [ ] The application of special defences to particular torts.

Introduction:
General defences

Once all the elements of any of the torts outlined in this book have been established, the only way in which a defendant may escape liability is to rely upon a defence.

Defences may be general, i.e. they apply to all torts (such as consent) or specific, i.e. they are applicable only to particular torts (such as self-defence which is a defence to trespass against the person). This chapter outlines the three main general defences: consent, contributory negligence and illegality and provides a table of the specific defences (as these are covered in more detail in the chapters dealing with the torts to which they apply).

   Awareness of the defences is crucial to understanding of tort law so they should not be overlooked as part of the revision process. Every defendant who faces liability will want to know whether they have a defence and, conceptually, the availability of defences is part of the way in which the boundaries of actionable tort are established. In practical terms, as any problem question could raise any of the general defences, it is not a topic that should be omitted from your revision.

Essay question advice

An essay may address the role of defences in tort generally or take a more narrow focus on a particular defence. The former question requires a good breadth of knowledge about the defences and an ability to see similarities and differences between them. The more specific type of question is likely to focus on the nature of a particular defence so you will need to make sure that you understand what each of the offences is trying to achieve. Remember that a defence is only needed if *prima facie* liability is established so there must be something about the circumstances covered by the defence that justify absolving a defendant from liability.

Problem question advice

It is difficult to envisage a problem question that deals with defences without dealing with some substantive tort as well: without liability there is no need for a defence. Keep the three main defences covered in this chapter in mind when analysing the facts of a problem question: did the claimant know there was a risk of the harm that occurred (consent); was he at fault in any way for the harm/damage that occurred (contributory negligence); was he involved in wrongdoing at the time that the harm/damage occurred (illegality)? Also be alert for specific defences arising in relation to particular torts and *never* 'borrow' a specific defence and use it in relation to a tort to which it is not applicable.

Sample question

Could you answer this question? Below is a typical problem question that could arise on this topic. Guidelines on answering the question are included at the end of the chapter, whilst a sample essay question and guidance on tackling it can be found on the companion website.

Problem question

Gerald is driving very slowly as he is towing a trailer carrying his donkeys, Nugget and Mulan. Danny, driving behind in a stolen car, gets impatient at the slow speed and overtakes Gerald on a blind bend, crashing into Tess, who was driving without a seatbelt as she did not want to crease her dress. Tess sustains serious head injuries as a result of the accident. Her passenger, Diane, who knew that the car had just failed its MOT due to faulty brakes, was also badly injured. Danny's passenger, Jack, who helped him steal the car, suffered a broken leg. Charlie, aged 8, heard the sound of the collision and ran into the road to see what was happening and was struck by Gerald's car, and sustained a fractured pelvis. Gerald was paying insufficient attention to the road as he was sending a text message to his girlfriend to tell her about the accident.

Identify the potential defendants and advise them as to what defences they could use to avoid or limit their liability.

■ Consent – *volenti non fit injuria*

KEY DEFINITION

The defence of **consent** is frequently referred to by the Latin term *volenti non fit injuria*. The literal translation of this is 'there can be no injury to one who consents' although it is often said to mean 'voluntary assumption of risk'.

The basis of this defence is that a person who consents to harm or consents to an activity which carries a risk of harm should not be able to hold the person who caused that harm liable in tort. Consent is a complete defence; if it is argued successfully, the defendant will not be liable for the claimant's loss.

Before the defence can be considered, it must be shown that the defendant has in fact committed a tort. Once this has been established, the defendant must then prove:

■ That the claimant had knowledge of the risk involved (the nature and extent of the risk); and
■ That the claimant willingly consented to accept that risk (a voluntary acceptance of that risk at the claimant's own free choice).

Knowledge of the risk

The first requirement of the defence is that the claimant must have had knowledge of the nature of the risk involved. This requires more than a vague awareness of danger but of a more specific knowledge of the type of risk involved in a particular activity. This is a subjective test.

KEY CASE

Morris v. *Murray* [1990] 3 All ER 801

Concerning: consent; knowledge of the risk

Facts

The claimant went drinking with a friend for some hours. The claimant's friend then suggested that they go on a joyride in his light aircraft. The aircraft, piloted by the claimant's friend took off down wind and uphill, in conditions of poor visibility, low cloud and drizzle when other flying at the aerodrome had been suspended. The aircraft crashed. The pilot was killed and the claimant was seriously injured in the crash. An autopsy on the pilot showed that he was more than three times the legal limit for driving. The claimant brought an action against the deceased's estate claiming damages for personal injury. The judge awarded him £130,900 damages. The estate appealed against the award.

Legal principle

The court applied a subjective test and held that the claimant was aware of the risk he was taking and therefore his claim against the deceased's estate was barred by the defence of consent.

As with any subjective test, you will have to find evidence of what the claimant knew or was thinking. This means that you should analyse the facts of a problem question carefully, looking for clues as to the claimant's awareness of the risk. Remember that any reference to 'obvious' risks will suggest to the examiner that you are applying an objective (reasonable person) test so avoid this and concentrate on the claimant's knowledge of the risk.

Consent of the claimant

The defendant must prove that the claimant freely consented to run the risk of injury. Knowledge of the risk is not the same as consent to running it.

Free consent implies that the claimant must have had a choice as to whether or not to accept the particular risk. The defence will therefore not succeed where the claimant had no choice but to accept the risk (*Smith* v. *Baker* [1891] AC 325) or where they lack the mental competence to agree: *Gillick* v. *West Norfolk and Wisbech AHA* [1986] AC 112.

There are certain categories of claimants who have received particular attention from the courts in terms of their consent to harm. Three of these, in particular, will be considered:

▍ Employees
▍ Passengers in vehicles
▍ Participants and spectators at sporting events.

Employees

Employees are in a difficult position. Their job may involve the risk of harm but the financial reality of life probably means that most people cannot consider the option of leaving their employment to avoid the risk of harm. It was held in *Smith* v. *Baker* [1891] AC 325 that continuing to work in a job that is known to carry risks cannot be taken as consent to the risk. For this reason, consent is rarely successful in relation to tortious claims by injured employees.

Passengers in vehicles

The courts have been reluctant to find that a person who is injured by poor driving, even if an obviously intoxicated driver, has consented to the injury (although there may be an issue of contributory negligence: see later in this Chapter). Section 149(3) of the Road Traffic Act 1988 makes it clear that the willing acceptance of the risk of negligence by a passenger does not absolve the driver of liability.

Participants and spectators

By voluntarily taking part in a sporting activity, individuals are deemed to have consented to the risks inherent in that sport. This will vary according to the nature of the activity: rugby carries more risk of injury than darts, for example. The general principle is that participation implies consent to injuries sustained during the course of normal play but not to unsporting behaviour that is in breach of the rules of the game: *Smoldon* v. *Whitworth and Nolan* [1997] PIQR 133.

Some sports, such as motor racing, carry risks to spectators. The general rule seems to be that spectators are deemed to have consented to the risk of harm arising from 'error of judgement or lapse of skill' by a participant but not to injuries caused by negligence: *Wooldridge* v. *Sumner* [1962] 2 All ER 978.

FURTHER THINKING

The judicial approach to consent in relation to participants and spectators at sporting events demonstrates its flexible nature. In other words, the courts will assess the situation and determine what level of risk of harm it is reasonable to deem an individual to have consented to by dint of their presence or participation.

For further insight into the complexities of the boundaries of consent in relation to sporting activities, see:

Fafinski, S., 'Consent and the Rules of the Game: the Interplay of Civil and Criminal Liability for Sporting Injuries' (2005) 69.5 *Journal of Criminal Law* 414

■ Illegality – *ex turpi causa non oritur actio*

KEY DEFINITION

The defence of **illegality** is frequently referred to by the Latin term *ex turpi causa non oritur actio* which means 'no action arises from a disgraceful claim'. In other words, if the claimant was knowingly engaged in an unlawful enterprise at the time he was injured, it would be contrary to public policy to allow his claim to succeed.

There must be a close connection between the injury sustained by the claimant and the criminal enterprise in which he is involved. For example, if two thieves were on their way to commit a burglary and one punched the other, there would be no defence of illegality to prevent a claim in tort for trespass to the person because the attack was unconnected with the planned criminal enterprise.

There is a fair degree of dissent amongst the case law as to the application of illegality. Some cases have taken a strong line and held that the claimant's participation in unlawful activity deprives him of any claim for injury sustained during the criminal enterprise:

- A burglar bitten by a guard dog had no claim due to illegality: *Cummings* v. *Granger* [1977] 1 All ER 104
- A claim for negligence against the police for injuries sustained by a prisoner who they failed to prevent from jumping out of a window was rejected on the basis of illegality: *Vellino* v. *Chief Constable of Greater Manchester Police* [2002] 3 All ER 78
- A claimant who started a fight but was severely injured by his opponent was prevented from claiming for the injuries sustained due to illegality: *Murphy* v. *Culhane* [1977] QB 74.

Although there is a fair amount of case law that shows that claimants have been unsuccessful because of illegality, there have been cases in which the courts have been reluctant to allow illegality to defeat the claim for damages:

KEY CASE

Revill v. *Newbury* [1996] 1 All ER 291

Concerning: illegality

Facts

The claimant went to steal property from a shed but the owner was in wait with a shotgun. The owner fired the gun in panic when the claimant started to enter the shed and he sustained serious injuries.

Legal principle

The court held that the claimant should not be deprived of a claim on the basis of illegality, saying that it was too 'far-reaching to deprive [the claimant] even of compensation for injury which he suffers and which otherwise he is entitled to recover at law'.

FURTHER THINKING

Although the defence of illegality was rejected in *Revill*, a defence of contributory negligence succeeded in reducing the damages he was awarded by two-thirds. Part of the reluctance of the courts to admit defences of consent and illegality arises from the fact that they entirely defeat a claim that has otherwise satisfied the requirements of the tort in question. By contrast, contributory negligence allows the claim to succeed but adjusts the level of damages awarded to reflect the claimant's responsibility for his own injury.

Awareness of the relationship between the defences and the policy considerations that have influenced the development of case law is necessary in

▶

order to write an essay on this topic. Further insight into these issues can be gained by reading:

Glofcheski, R.A., 'Plaintiff's Illegality as a Bar to Recovery of Personal Injury' (1999) *Legal Studies* vol. 19, pp. 6–23

■ Contributory negligence

KEY STATUTORY PROVISION

Law Reform (Contributory Negligence) Act 1945, section 1(1)

Where any person suffers damage as the result partly of his own fault and partly of the fault of any other person ... a claim in respect of that damage shall not be defeated ... but the damages recoverable in respect thereof shall be reduced to such an extent as the court thinks just and equitable having regard to the claimant's share in the responsibility for the damage.

Unlike consent and illegality, contributory negligence is not a complete defence but a partial defence that reduces the level of damages payable to the claimant. It applies when the claimant's carelessness has in some way caused, or contributed to, his own injuries.

EXAM TIP

Although this defence is phrased in terms of negligence, this should not be taken as meaning that it is only a defence in relation to the tort of negligence. The reference to negligence relates to the claimant's fault in contributing to his own injury, not the means by which the defendant caused him injury so it is applicable to most torts (section 4).

Claimant's damage

The requirement that the claimant has suffered damage includes, but is not limited to, death and personal injury (section 4). As such, it would include any other loss for which damages could be awarded in tort such as damage to property and economic loss.

Claimant's fault

In order for a defence of contributory negligence to succeed, it must be established that the claimant failed to take care of his own safety in a way that at least partially caused the damage that he suffered.

Jones v. *Livox Quarries* [1952] 2 QB 608

Concerning: foreseeability of harm

Facts

The claimant was injured at work when two quarrying vehicles collided. The claimant was sat on the back of one of the vehicles at the time of the collision, without the driver's knowledge and in contravention of the explicit prohibition on doing so.

Legal principle

It was held that this did amount to contributory negligence as the claimant 'ought to have foreseen that, if he did not act as a reasonable, prudent man, he might be hurt himself'.

Therefore, the injury which the claimant suffered must have been a foreseeable consequence of his own behaviour even though the injury was caused by the defendant.

EXAM TIP

The essence of contributory negligence is that it takes into account the conduct of both the claimant and the defendant so remember to examine the behaviour of both parties. In particular, ask 'did the claimant do anything to put himself at risk of suffering this injury or to increase the seriousness of his injuries?', as, if so, this is a good indication that contributory negligence will be established.

Standard of care

The standard of care is that of the reasonably prudent person. In other words, a defence of contributory negligence will succeed if it can be established that the claimant failed to recognise that he was jeopardising his own safety if this would have been obvious to the ordinary person.

Children

There is an exception to this in relation to children as the courts have acknowledged that children are less likely to recognise the risks inherent in their conduct than adults.

Gough v. Thorne [1966] 3 All ER 398

Concerning: age of the claimant

Facts

The 13-year-old claimant was struck by a car as she was crossing the road. Her view had been obscured by a lorry but the driver had indicated that it was clear to cross the road. Unfortunately, a car swerved past the lorry and struck the claimant and the issue was whether her damages should be reduced on the basis of contributory negligence.

Legal principle

The court held that there was no contributory negligence as the claimant had done all that could be expected of a child of her age:

> A very young child cannot be guilty of contributory negligence. An older child may be; but it depends on the circumstances. A judge should only find a child guilty of contributory negligence if he or she is of such an age as reasonably to be expected to take precautions for his or her own safety; and then he or she is only to be found guilty if blame is to be attached to him or her (*per* Lord Denning).

The key question in relation to child claimants is whether their behaviour showed a level of care for their own safety that was appropriate for their age:

- An 11-year-old claimant was injured after being struck by a car whilst playing with a football in the middle of a busy road: a 75% reduction in damages for contributory negligence because this risk would be obvious to an ordinary 11-year-old (*Morales* v. *Eccleston* [1991] RTR 151)
- A nine-year-old claimant suffered serious burns after setting fire to some petrol supplied by the defendants. This was not contributory negligence as he was not of an age where he would appreciate the danger of playing with petrol (*Yachuk* v. *Oliver Blais* [1949] AC 386).

REVISION NOTE

Further evidence of differential standards being applied to children can be seen in relation to occupiers' liability. You might find it useful to revist Chapter 6 to refresh your memory about the approach taken there and consider how it compares to contributory negligence. This would be particularly useful to ensure that you were prepared for a question involving child claimants.

Rescuers

The objective standard of care is also modified in relation to rescue situations where it becomes the standard of the reasonable rescuer: only if a rescuer has shown 'wholly unreasonable disregard for his or her own safety' will there be a finding of contributory negligence: *Baker* v. *TE Hopkins & Son Ltd* [1959] 3 All ER 225.

Emergency situations

It is also recognised that a person faced with sudden peril may respond in a way that does not seem to be the best course of action when viewed with the benefit of hindsight. A person acting 'in the agony of the moment' is not expected to take time to weigh up the risk of his action and this is taken into account in relation to contributory negligence. In *Jones* v. *Boyce* (1816) 1 Stark 492, it was held that the question is whether the claimant's actions were reasonable in the context of the dangerous situation in which he was placed.

Apportionment of blame

If a defendant establishes contributory negligence, the court will look at the contribution of both parties to the harm suffered by the claimant and apportion a percentage of responsibility to each party. The claimant's damages will then be reduced by that percentage. In *Stapley* v. *Gypsum Mines Ltd* [1953] 2 All ER 470, it was held that there are two factors to be taken into account when deciding how to apportion blame:

- **Causation**: the extent to which the claimant's own behaviour caused or contributed to his injuries
- **Culpability**: the relative blameworthiness of the claimant and defendant for the injuries sustained by the claimant.

Notice that the focus is on the claimant's contribution to his injuries. This is different from a requirement that he contributed to the accident that caused the injuries. The claimant may be entirely blameless in terms of causing the accident in which he was injured but may have his damages reduced for contributory negligence if he has contributed to his own injuries.

Froom v. *Butcher* [1975] 3 All ER 520

Concerning: reduction for contribution to injury

Facts

The claimant was injured when the car in which she was a passenger was struck by an oncoming vehicle, driven dangerously by the defendant. The claimant was not wearing a seatbelt and the issue was whether this could amount to contributory negligence.

Legal principle

It was held that contributory negligence was concerned with the cause of the claimant's injuries, not the cause of the accident in which the injuries were sustained. The injury was caused in part by the defendant's bad driving and in part by the claimant's failure to wear a seatbelt and, as such, she had contributed to her own injuries and a reduction in the quantum of damages was appropriate.

The Court of Appeal went on to establish a scale of reductions based upon failure to wear a seatbelt:

- Injuries would have been avoided altogether if a seatbelt had been worn: 25% reduction
- Injuries would have been less severe if a seatbelt had been worn: 15% reduction
- Injuries would have been the same even if a seatbelt had been worn: no reduction.

As *Froom* v. *Butcher* makes clear, the focus of attention must not be on the claimant's behaviour in isolation but in how the claimant's behaviour has contributed to his injuries. If the claimant has behaved badly but would have been just as seriously

Figure 11.1

Iestyn is cycling home from work through busy traffic. He is not wearing his cycle helmet because he has a headache. A car, driving erratically, clips the wheel of his bicycle and Iestyn falls, hitting his head on the kerb and suffering a broken arm	Contribution to the injuries	Iestyn makes no contribution to the accident. His failure to wear his cycle helmet has contributed to his injuries as his head would have been less badly injured had he been wearing it. A reduction in damages on the basis of contributory negligence is likely
Iestyn is coming home from the pub after drinking heavily. He finds it hard to steer and is weaving about. A car rounds the bend at a high speed on the wrong side of the road. It knocks Iestyn off his bicycle and he sustains serious injuries in the accident	No contribution to the injuries	Although Iestyn is being careless in the way that he is riding his bicycle, this makes no contribution to his injuries. It is likely that the accident would have occurred in the same way and resulted in the same injuries irrespective of his drunkenness and inability to steer his bicycle

injured if he had been behaving in an impeccable fashion, there will be no contributory negligence; see Figure 11.1.

Specific defences

Unlike the general defences outlined in this chapter, those in the table are limited in application to a particular tort. They are listed here for the sake of completeness but you will find a more detailed account in the chapter dealing with the relevant tort.

Tort	Defences
Occupiers' liability (Chapter 6)	Warning notices
Nuisance (Chapter 7)	Prescription
	Statutory authority
Trespass to land (Chapter 8)	Contractual licence
	Lawful authority
	Necessity
False imprisonment: trespass to the person (Chapter 9)	Reasonable condition for release
	Lawful arrest
	Medical detention
Assault and battery: trespass to the person (Chapter 9)	Lawful authority
	Self-defence
	Parental authority
	Consent
	Necessity
Defamation (Chapter 10)	Privilege
	Innocent publication
	Consent
	Justification
	Fair comment
	Offer of amends

Chapter summary:
Putting it all together

☐ Can you tick all the points from the revision checklist at the beginning of this chapter?

☐ Take the **end-of-chapter quiz** on the companion website.

☐ Test your knowledge of the cases with the **revision flashcards** on the website.

☐ Attempt the problem question from the beginning of the chapter using the guidelines below.

☐ Go to the companion website to try out other questions.

Answer guidelines

See the problem question at the start of the chapter. A diagram illustrating how to structure your answer is available on the website.

1 One of the key difficulties of tackling a question such as this comes in identifying the appropriate defendant in relation to each claimant. This is particularly complex here as Gerald would not initially attract any liability (do not be tempted into considering whether driving slowly, i.e. taking extra care, would amount to negligence) but is likely to have done so at a later stage in relation to Charlie. Time taken in analysing the facts will help to avoid confusion:

▪ **Tess**: it will be straightforward to establish that Danny's driving amounted to actionable negligence so the issue will be contributory negligence as Tess was not wearing a seatbelt.

▪ **Diane**: would you consider that she has an action against Danny (who caused the accident) or Tess (who was driving the car in which she was a passenger)? The information about the faulty brakes in Tess' car is a bit of a red herring because there is no suggestion that her driving was responsible for the accident. It would be important to point this out and focus on Diane's potential action against Danny.

▪ **Jack**: again, it will be straightforward to establish a claim in negligence given the poor quality of Danny's driving. Make sure that you stick to an appropriate structure of (1) establishing liability and (2) considering the availability of a defence. This means that the question of Jack's collusion in unlawful activity should arise at the second stage (there is potential to consider consent and illegality). Do not make the mistake of arguing that Jack's role in stealing the car means that he has no claim in tort: he has a claim but his contribution to events may give Danny a defence.

- **Charlie**: the focus moves to Gerald as a defendant here as he is not paying attention to the road and has struck Charlie. Remember that the standard of care to protect oneself from harm is modified in relation to children.

Make your answer really stand out

- Once you have untangled the facts, this is quite a straightforward answer. Although the focus is clearly on defences, make sure that you do not skimp on establishing liability – remember, there is no need for a defence unless *prima facie* liability is established so that should always be the starting point of your answer.
- Explaining your decision to take a particular slant on the facts can demonstrate your understanding and really impress your examiner. For example, it would be useful to include an explanation (as stated above) of why Danny is the appropriate defendant in relation to Diane, rather than Tess who was knowingly driving a car with defective brakes.
- Remember that contributory negligence requires that the claimant caused or contributed to his own injuries, not necessarily to the accident that led to the injuries. This is exemplified by the blameless driver/passenger who is not wearing a seatbelt. Try to incorporate the *Froom* v. *Butcher* calculation for the reduction in damages.

12
Remedies

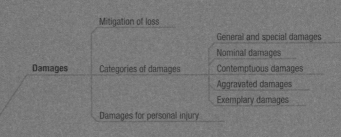

Damages

Mitigation of loss

Categories of damages
- General and special damages
- Nominal damages
- Contemptuous damages
- Aggravated damages
- Exemplary damages

Damages for personal injury

Remedies

Injunctions
- *Quia timet* injunction
- Interim injunction
- Final injunction
- Equitable maxims

Revision checklist

What you need to know:

- [ ] The circumstances in which damages are awarded
- [ ] The distinction between the different categories of damages
- [ ] The different types of injunction and their application
- [ ] The relationship between damages and injunctions.

Introduction:
Remedies

This chapter focuses on the two main remedies available in tort: damages and injunctions.

These remedies are of general application and are supplemented by some specific remedies that are available only to particular torts, such as abatement in relation to the tort of nuisance. Most claimants who have suffered a tortious wrong are concerned either to prevent the continuation or repetition of the problem (injunction) or to obtain financial recompense for the harm they have suffered (damages). Damages are a legal remedy that are available 'as of right' to a successful claimant, i.e. he is entitled to an award of damages, whereas injunctions are equitable remedies so are available at the court's discretion; a successful claimant will not automatically be granted an injunction.

Remedies are frequently omitted for tort revision. This is unfortunate as it is one of the two key issues for a client who is a claimant and defendant in a tort case: (1) will I be successful or liable? and (2) what will I get (if I win) or have to pay (if I lose)? Moreover, an understanding of the heads of damage will help you to identify potential causes of action so this will enhance your ability to deal with liability in relation to the substantive torts that you have studied.

Essay question advice

An essay on remedies would require not only a detailed knowledge of the types of damages and injunctions and their application but also of the policy underlying their use. These issues are not complex but do require careful attention to detail, for example in providing a correct outline of the different types of damages.

Sample question

Could you answer this question? Below is a typical problem question that could arise on this topic. Guidelines on answering the question are included at the end of the chapter, whilst a sample essay question and guidance on tackling it can be found on the companion website.

Problem question

Jack is a freelance journalist who is determined to obtain photographs of a notoriously reclusive celebrity, Mrs P. He pitches a tent on land adjoining Mrs P's home so that he can monitor her movements. The owner, Monty, asks him to leave on several occasions. Jack does so only after accidentally setting fire to a barn on Monty's property with a discarded cigarette. Abandoning his attempts to photograph Mrs P at home, he decides to catch her unawares at the gym. The gym is exclusive but Jack plans to pose as a prospective member in order to get a tour of the premises. He is unable to find a parking space so he leaves his car parked on Charlie's lawn. During this tour of the gym, the manager, Mabel, spots Jack taking photographs and asks him to leave. Enraged, Jack pushes Mabel into a nearby cupboard and locks the door. She is released four hours later when her cries are heard by a cleaner. Frustrated by his failure to get a photograph of Mrs P, Jack sells a fabricated story to a national newspaper that alleges that X is a regular user of cocaine.

Discuss the remedies available to the victims of Jack's tortious behaviour.

Damages

Damages are the primary remedy available in tort. The principle is that the award of damages should return the claimant to the position that they would have been in had the tort not occurred. This is not always straightforward as some tortious harms are less amenable to quantification than others; for example, if the defendant's trespass to land damages the claimant's wall, the cost of repairing or replacing the wall can be calculated but other sorts of harm are less easy to represent in financial terms. There are three basic situations:

▌ Harm, loss or injury that is amenable to quantification such as damage to property
▌ Harm, loss or injury that is harder to quantify typically involving personal injury
▌ Torts which are actionable *per se*, i.e. there is no requirement of harm where the damages represent the wrong arising from interference with the claimant's legal interest. For example, damages for trespass to the person reflect the interference with the claimant's right to bodily integrity and freedom from interference.

In addition to the difficulties of calculating the value of certain kinds of damage, there are also other factors to take into account such as the claimant's duty to mitigate their loss and situations in which the courts award damages that go beyond mere recompense for loss.

Mitigation of loss

A claimant who suffers loss as a result of the defendant's tort is entitled to an award of damages to ensure that they are not 'out of pocket'. However, a claimant must take reasonable steps to ensure that the losses that they are claiming are kept to a minimum. For example, a claimant who is not able to continue in his usual employment due to the defendant's conduct must seek reasonable alternative employment in order to mitigate his loss.

Categories of damages
General and special damages

These are illustrated in the table on p166.

Special damages	General damages
Those which are capable of being calculated at the time of the trial and which are presented to the court in a form of calculation	Those which are not capable of being calculated at the time of trial so are left to the court to quantify
Loss of earnings before trial	Loss of future earnings
Medical expenses prior to trial	Cost of future medical expenses
Damage to property, e.g. loss of a vehicle in an accident	Pain and suffering

Nominal damages

These damages are awarded when the claimant's rights have been infringed but little harm has been caused. This type of damages is frequently awarded in relation to torts which are actionable *per se* and cases in which the primary aim of the claimant was to obtain an injunction:

- The defendant abandoned a broken-down car on the claimant's land. There is liability for trespass to land but little actual damage.
- The defendant persistently parks his car on the claimant's land. The claimant is concerned to obtain an injunction to prevent him from doing so rather than obtaining damages.

Contemptuous damages

These damages are also awarded when the level of harm caused is low. They differ from nominal damages in that the court feels that the action should not have been brought (even though the claimant has been successful in establishing the elements of a tort). To reflect the court's view that the claimant was wrong to bring a claim, an award of contemptuous damages is extremely low, often the lowest value currency available: 1p damages.

Aggravated damages

These damages are awarded over and above the damages that are necessary to return the claimant to the position that he would have been in had the tort not occurred. They are additional sums of money to reflect that the initial harm was made worse by some aggravating factor, often injury to feelings or anxiety and distress caused by the defendant. As such, they are often awarded in cases involving defamation and trespass to the person.

Thompson v. *Metropolitan Police Comr* **[1997] 2 All ER 762**

Concerning: aggravated damages

Facts

The claimant was lawfully arrested for a driving offence but the police used excessive force to place her in a cell.

Legal principle

It was held that additional damages should be awarded when there are aggravating features about the case that mean that the claimant would not otherwise receive sufficient compensation. The court held that aggravating features 'can include humiliating circumstances ... or any conduct of those responsible ... which shows that they had behaved in a high-handed, insulting, malicious or oppressive manner'.

Exemplary damages

There is often some confusion about the distinction between aggravated damages (above) and exemplary damages as the latter is also an additional award that reflects the court's disapproval of the defendant's conduct. There is, however, a crucial distinction between the two types of damages as Figure 12.1 illustrates.

Figure 12.1

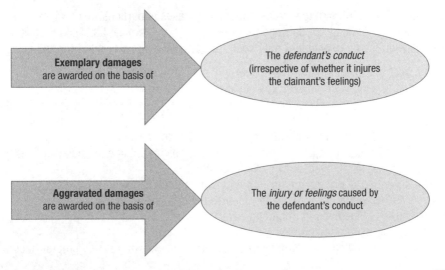

Exemplary damages are awarded on the basis of → The *defendant's conduct* (irrespective of whether it injures the claimant's feelings)

Aggravated damages are awarded on the basis of → The *injury or feelings* caused by the defendant's conduct

Rookes v. *Barnard* [1964] AC 1129

Concerning: distinction between aggravated and exemplary damages

Facts

After a disagreement, the claimant left his union. The defendant, an unpaid union official, told the claimant's employer that there would be a strike unless the claimant was dismissed. Following his dismissal, the claimant brought a civil action founded in conspiracy against the defendant and others.

Legal principle

The House of Lords considered the distinction between aggravated and exemplary damages. It was held that the purpose of aggravated damages was to compensate the claimant for loss or harm suffered whilst the purpose of exemplary damages was to punish the defendant for unacceptable behaviour and deter others from similar behaviour. It was held that there are three situations that justify the imposition of exemplary damages:

(1) Oppressive, arbitrary or unconstitutional action by the servants of the government.
(2) Cases where the defendant is calculated to make a profit that will exceed the compensation otherwise payable to the claimant.
(3) In situations where exemplary damages are explicitly authorised by statute.

Damages for personal injury

The quantification of damages in personal injury cases is particularly complex due to the wide range of heads of damage that may arise. For example, a person who is seriously injured in an accident may wish to recover for some or all of the following:

■ The cost of replacing personal property damaged in the accident
■ Loss of earnings (1) between the accident and trial and (2) after the trial
■ Loss of earning capacity if he is unable to perform the same level of work after the accident
■ Damages for pain and suffering (before and after the accident)
■ Damages for loss of amenity if he is no longer able to engage in social and leisure pursuits that he enjoyed prior to the accident
■ The costs of any private medical care (a claimant is entitled to private treatment even if NHS treatment is available) incurred before and after the trial
■ The expenses involved in obtaining care assistance in the home if his injuries leave him unable to care for himself
■ The costs of having his home adapted to his needs, i.e. ramps, lowered surfaces.

FURTHER THINKING

This list of potential heads of damage gives an indication of the complexity of a personal injury claim, particularly as some of the losses are clearly not amenable to mathematical calculation (non-pecuniary losses). The intricacies of the calculation of personal injury claims is beyond the scope of this revision guide so if this is covered in detail on your syllabus you will need to consult a specialist text that deals with the issue, such as:

Cane, P. (1999) *Atiyah's Accidents, Compensation and the Law*, 6th edn, Cambridge: Cambridge University Press

▉ Injunctions

An injunction is a discretionary remedy which takes the form of a court order that requires that the defendant behave in a particular way. This can take two forms:

- ▉ *Prohibitory*: the most common form of injunction which requires the defendant to refrain from doing something; in other words, to stop committing the tort that he is committing;
- ▉ *Mandatory*: these compel the defendant to take a particular action to rectify the situation that has arisen due to his tortious behaviour. As they require positive action, they are considered to be an onerous burden to impose upon the defendant and are relatively uncommon and in strictly limited circumstances:

KEY CASE

Redland Bricks Ltd v. *Morris* [1970] AC 652

Concerning: conditions for granting a mandatory injunction

Facts

The claimants (respondents) and defendants (appellants) owned adjoining land. The appellants (Redland Bricks) used their land to quarry clay and their activities caused the land belonging to the respondents (Morris), who were market gardeners, to subside. Further slips were predicted that would make the respondents' land unworkable as a market garden. The estimated cost of remedying the slippage was £30,000, which greatly exceeded the value of the respondents' land (£12,000). Notwithstanding this, the trial judge granted a mandatory injunction requiring that the damage be remedied.

Legal principle

The House of Lords dismissed the appeal and overturned the injunction. As the cost of remedial action would exceed the value of the land, it was not appropriate to impose a mandatory injunction. Four criteria were:

▶

(1) A strong possibility of substantial damage in the future.
(2) Pecuniary remedies, i.e. damages, would be inadequate.
(3) The defendants have behaved 'wantonly or unreasonably'.
(4) The injunction must be capable of reflecting exactly what the defendant was compelled to do.

Although injunctions can be used in relation to any tort, they are most common in relation to problems that are likely to continue so are used most frequently in relation to nuisance, trespass to land, harassment and defamation. Failure to comply with an injunction amounts to a contempt of court and may be punishable by a fine or imprisonment.

There are three kinds of injunction that vary according to the time at which they are obtained in relation to the commission of the tort, see Figure 12.2.

Figure 12.2

Prior to the tort
If the claimant has good grounds to believe that a tort will be committed, he may apply for a *quia timet* injunction

When the tort is committed
The claimant can apply to the court for an *interim injunction* to stop the tort before the trial to resolve the main issue

After the tort is committed
The claimant may seek a *final injunction* to prevent the reoccurrence of the tort

Tort occurs

Quia timet injunction

This is an injunction which is obtained prior to the commission of a tort in order to prevent its occurrence. For example, a person who knows that a neighbour plans to hold a noisy event may wish to apply for a *quia timet* injunction to prevent its occurrence. Such injunctions are only granted if:

■ There is a high likelihood that a tortious event will occur;

■ This event would cause significant damage or disruption to the claimant; and
■ The defendant will not desist unless an injunction is granted.

Interim injunction

This is also known as an interlocutory injunction and may be granted once an action has been commenced pending the full hearing of the issue. In other words, if a claimant initiates an action in nuisance, there will be a lapse of time before the claim is heard so the claimant may seek an interim injunction to prevent the continuation of the nuisance until the matter is resolved. The guidelines for granting an interim injunction have been outlined by the House of Lords:

KEY CASE

American Cyanamid v. *Ethicon* [1975] AC 396

Concerning: conditions for granting an interim injunction

Facts

The case concerned a dispute between two companies both concerned with the manufacture and supply of disposable sutures. The claimant sought an interim injunction to prevent an alleged breach of patent law.

Legal principle

The House of Lords outlined the conditions that must exist for an interim injunction to be granted:

(1) The claimant must establish that there is a serious issue to be tried.
(2) That the balance of convenience favoured the grant of an injunction, i.e. whether damages would be an adequate remedy at the end of the trial must be balanced against the consideration of whether damages would be sufficient to compensate the defendant for the enforced cessation of lawful activity if the claim was unsuccessful.
(3) If there is no imbalance, the status quo must be preserved.

The reference to the balance of convenience (Figure 12.3) between the parties gets to the heart of the difficulty associated with the grant of interim injunctions. As the case has not been heard, the court is not sure whether or not a tort is actually being committed.

It is for this reason that a claimant must undertake to pay damages to the defendant if an interim injunction is granted but there is eventually found to be no liability in tort.

Figure 12.3

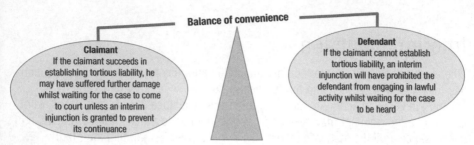

Final injunctions

The usual remedy in tort is damages and a claimant will not be granted an injunction unless he is able to establish that damages would not be an adequate remedy.

FURTHER THINKING

In situations where there is a risk of ongoing tortious behaviour, damages will not be adequate. For example, a financial award would do little for a claimant whose sleep is repeatedly disturbed by noise emanating from a neighbouring building (private nuisance, see Chapter 7) or a claimant whose everyday life was blighted by persistent harassment from the defendant (harassment, see Chapter 9). To award damages in such a case would be the equivalent of allowing the defendant to purchase the right to commit a tort.

Equitable maxims

As injunctions are equitable remedies, their availability is limited by general equitable principles. Therefore, claimants must ensure that the circumstances of their case do not offend against key equitable maxims, as the table below illustrates.

Equitable maxim	Meaning in relation to injunctions
Equity does nothing in vain	An injunction will not be granted if it would be ineffective, e.g. if the defendant would not be able to comply with its terms
Delay defeats equity	A claimant who has not acted promptly in bringing an action will not be awarded an injunction against the defendant
He who seeks equity must do equity	Equity is concerned with fairness thus a claimant who seeks an injunction must not have encouraged the defendant in his tortious behaviour or acquiesced to its existence

▌Chapter summary:
▌Putting it all together

☐ Can you tick all the points from the revision checklist at the beginning of this chapter?

☐ Take the **end-of-chapter quiz** on the companion website.

☐ Test your knowledge of the cases with the **revision flashcards** on the website.

☐ Attempt the problem question from the beginning of the chapter using the guidelines below.

☐ Go to the companion website to try out other questions.

Answer guidelines

See the problem question at the start of the chapter. A diagram illustrating how to structure your answer is available on the website.

1 The question specifically instructs you to concentrate on remedies. This means that there would be little credit to be gained in spending time outlining Jack's liability. This will not always be the case, it will depend on the wording of the question. If this question had specified 'discuss Jack's liability and any defences available to his victims' there would be a need to get a more even balance between liability and defences in your answer. Make a point of double-checking the instructions that accompany the question to ensure that you know what is required of you.

2 As always with a problem question involving multiple events/parties, you should take time to unravel the facts to ensure that you have a clear idea of what issues need to be addressed before you start to write. In relation to this question, you could make a list that looked something like this:

   ▪ **Jack/Monty – trespass to land**: pitching tent, potential for an injunction to prevent continuation, little merit to an award of damages as no harm/injury apparent.

   ▪ **Jack/Monty – negligence**: setting fire to barn, most appropriate remedy is damages which would be quantifiable at the time of trial so are special damages (which would require definition).

   ▪ **Jack/Mrs P – harassment**: his surveillance of her home, most appropriate remedy is an injunction as she is concerned to prevent any further harassment.

   ▪ **Jack/Charlie – trespass to land**: parking his car, transient trespass with no evidence of harm thus likely to obtain only nominal damages (define) or possible contemptuous damages (define) if the judge feels that he should not have made a claim, possibility of injunction but little to suggest that there would be repetition.

■ **Jack/Mabel – trespass to land**: Jack refuses to leave when asked to do so but is there any point in making a claim on this basis (see Charlie)?

■ **Jack/Mabel – false imprisonment**: invites a discussion of the distinction between exemplary and aggravated damages.

■ **Jack/Mrs P – defamation**: again, appropriate to discuss aggravated damages (due to the distress caused) and exemplary damages (given that his aim is to make a profit).

Make your answer really stand out

■ As you will see, once you have untangled the facts, the issues that need to be addressed are not difficult. The key skill involved in problem questions involving a lot of issues and tangled facts is the ability to create order out of chaos. Presenting an organised answer that states each issue clearly and is easy for the examiner to follow will gain a great deal of credit.

■ Although the question requires a focus on remedies, it would be appropriate to devote one or two sentences to explaining the nature of the liability involved in Jack's conduct to demonstrate your wide knowledge of a range of torts. Remember, though, that it would be counter-productive to get carried away and include too much detail.

■ The distinction between aggravated and exemplary damages is tricky so careful revision of *Rookes* v. *Barnard* is needed.

Conclusion

By using this revision guide to direct your work, you should now have a good knowledge and understanding of the way in which the various aspects of the law of tort work in isolation and the many ways in which they are interrelated. What's more, you should have acquired the necessary skills and techniques to demonstrate that knowledge and understanding in the examination, regardless of whether the questions are presented to you in essay or problem form.

TEST YOURSELF

☐ Look at the summary checklist of the points below. Are you happy that you can now tick them all? If not, go back to the particular chapter and work through the material again. If you are still struggling, **seek help** from your tutor

☐ Go to the companion website and revisit the interactive **quizzes** provided for each chapter.

☐ Make sure you can recall the **legal principles** of the key cases and statutory provisions that you have revised.

☐ Go to the companion website and test your knowledge of cases and terms with the **revision flashcards**.

Summary checklist

Do you know:

▌ The composite elements required to establish negligence?
▌ The definition of the legal duty of care?
▌ Established and special duty of care situations?
▌ General and special standards of care?
▌ How to determine the standard of care and prove breach of duty?
▌ How to explain factual causation and apply the 'but for' test?
▌ How to identify and address the problems posed by multiple causes?
▌ The difficulties of establishing a 'lost chance'?
▌ The meaning of *novus actus interveniens* and its impact on causation?

- The principles and policies involved in remoteness of damage?
- The definition of economic loss and the limited circumstances under which it may be recoverable?
- The changes to the extent of economic loss introduced by *Anns*, *Junior Books* and *Murphy*?
- The principles of negligent misstatement?
- The definition of psychiatric injury and how it applies to primary and secondary victims?
- The requirements that must be satisfied for vicarious liability to arise?
- The tests used to distinguish between an employee and an independent contractor?
- The meaning of course of employment and the relevance of 'a frolic of one's own?
- The implications of failure to obey instructions or the commission of an intentionally wrongful act?
- The ways in which an employer may recover the cost of paying damages to the claimant from the employee?
- The scope of the common law duty to ensure the safety of employees?
- The operation of the law in relation to safety of premises, plant, system of work and competency of staff?
- The elements of the tort of breach of statutory duty?
- The tests used to determine whether a breach is actionable?
- The meaning of key terms such as occupier, visitor, premises and trespasser?
- The scope of the duty established under the Occupiers' Liability Act 1957?
- The implications of the Occupiers' Liability Act 1984 in relation to liability for trespassers?
- The defences available to an occupier and the ability to limit or exclude liability?
- The liability for dangers created by independent contractors on land occupied by others?
- The elements of private nuisance and its role in protecting rights in land including key concepts concerning the unreasonable use of land such as malice, the sensitivity of the claimant and the character of the neighbourhood?
- The role of public nuisance and the relevance of key concepts such as the class of people affected and the requirement for special damage?
- The distinction between private and public nuisance and their relationship with other property torts such as trespass to land?
- The nature and operation of defences and the availability of remedies with regard to nuisance?
- The nature of trespass to land and its composite elements?
- Definitions of key concepts such as land, possession and trespass *ab initio*?
- The relationship between trespass to land and other torts such as nuisance?
- The availability of defences and remedies with regard to trespass to land?
- The nature of trespass to the person as a broad category?
- Definitions of the individual torts that comprise trespass to the person?
- The relationship between trespass to the person and other torts?

■ The availability and operation of defences and remedies with regard to trespass to the person?

■ Definitions of libel and slander and the distinction between them?

■ The elements of defamation?

■ The availability and operation of the defences with regard to defamation?

■ The underlying tension between an individual's right to privacy and another's right to freedom of expression?

■ The elements and availability of the three general defences?

■ The relationship between the absolute defences and the partial defence of contributory negligence?

■ The relevance of particular categories of claimants such as children, employees and passengers in motor vehicles?

■ The application of special defences to particular torts?

■ The circumstances in which damages are awarded?

■ The distinction between the different categories of damages?

■ The different types of injunction and their application?

■ The relationship between damages and injunctions?

Glossary of terms

Key definitions

Assault   'An act which causes another person to apprehend the infliction of immediate, unlawful force on his person: *Collins* v. *Wilcox* [1984] 3 All ER 374 *per* Lord Goff

Battery   'The intentional and direct application of force to another person' (Rogers, W.V.H. (2002) *Winfield and Jolowicz on Tort*, 16th edn, London: Sweet & Maxwell, p. 71)

Consent   A defence which is frequently referred to by the Latin term *volenti non fit injuria*. The literal translation of this is 'there can be no injury to one who consents' although it is often said to mean 'voluntary assumption of risk'

Control test   Distinguishes an employee and an independent contractor on the basis of whether the employer had the right to control the nature of the work done and, most importantly, how it must be done: *Yewen* v. *Noakes* (1880) 6 QBD 530

Defamation   'The publication of a[n untrue] statement which reflects on a person's reputation and tends to lower him in the estimation of right-thinking members of society generally or tends to make them shun or avoid him' (Rogers, W.V.H. (2002) *Winfield and Jolowicz on Tort*, 16th edn, London: Sweet & Maxwell, p. 405)

Defamatory statement   One that is 'calculated to injure the reputation of another, by exposing them to hatred, contempt or ridicule': *Parmiter* v. *Coupland* (1840) 6 M&W 105; and which tends to 'lower the [claimant] in the estimation of right-thinking members of society: *Sim* v. *Stretch* (1936) 52 TLR 669

Economic loss   Financial loss which is not attributable to physical harm caused to the claimant or his property. It includes loss of profits, loss of trade and loss of investment revenue

False imprisonment	'The infliction of bodily restraint which is not expressly or impliedly authorised by the law' (Rogers, W.V.H. (2002) *Winfield and Jolowicz on Tort*, 16th edn, London: Sweet & Maxwell, p. 81)
'A frolic of his own'	A phrase used to describe conduct that falls outside the course of employment, being something that the employee has done within working time that is unrelated to his work and undertaken on his own account: *Joel* v. *Morrison* (1834) 6 C&P 501
Illegality	A defence which is frequently referred to by the Latin term *ex turpi causa non oritur actio* which means 'no action arises from a disgraceful claim'. In other words, if the claimant was knowingly engaged in an unlawful enterprise at the time he was injured, it would be contrary to public policy to allow his claim to succeed
Joint liability	Arises if two or more people cause harm/damage to the same claimant when they are (1) engaged in a joint enterprise; (2) one party authorises the tort of the other; and (3) one party is vicariously liable for the torts of the other
Negligence	Breach of a legal duty to take care which results in damage to the claimant (Rogers, W.V.H. (2002) *Winfield and Jolowicz on Tort*, 16th edn, London: Sweet & Maxwell, p. 103)
Novus actus interveniens	A Latin phrase which means 'a new act intervenes'
Occupier	A person who exercises an element of control over premises: *Wheat* v. *E. Lacon & Co Ltd* [1966] 1 All ER 582
Organisation test	Distinguishes between a *contract of service* whereby 'a man is employed as part of the business and his work is done as an integral part of the business' and a *contract for services* whereby 'work, although done for the business, is not integrated into it but is only accessory to it': *Stevenson, Jordan and Harrison Ltd* v. *Macdonald and Evans* [1952] 1 TLR 101
Private nuisance	'The unreasonable use of man of his land to the detriment of his neighbour': *Miller* v. *Jackson* [1977] 3 All ER 338
Public nuisance	'Materially affects the reasonable comfort and convenience of life of a class of Her Majesty's subjects': *A-G* v. *PYA Quarries Ltd* [1957] 2 QB 169 *per* Romer LJ
Res ipsa loquitur	A Latin phrase which means 'the thing speaks for itself'
Several liability	Occurs in all cases that do not fall within *joint liability* but

where more than one defendant has caused harm/damage to the claimant

Trespass to land A direct and 'unjustified interference with the possession of land ... whether or not the entrant knows that he is trespassing' (Rogers, W.V.H. (2002) *Winfield and Jolowicz on Tort*, 16th edn, London: Sweet & Maxwell, p. 487)

Trespasser 'Someone who goes on the land without invitation of any sort and whose presence is either unknown to the proprietor or, if known, is practically objected to': *Robert Addie & Sons (Collieries) Ltd* v. *Dumbreck* [1929] AC 358

Index

ambulance service, duty of care 10

arrest, lawful, as defence for false imprisonment 130

assault 124–8
  defences 126–8
    consent 127
    lawful authority 126
    necessity 128
    parental authority 127
    self-defence 127
  definition 124
  intentional act 124–5
  reasonable fear 126

battery 122–4
  defences 126–8
    consent 127
    lawful authority 126
    necessity 128
    parental authority 127
    self-defence 127
  definition 122
  direct application of force 123
  intentional use of force 122–3
  level of force 123–4

blame, apportionment, and contributory negligence 157–9

breach of duty and negligence 10–22
  establishing – summary 11
  proving 19–22
    Civil Evidence Act 21–2
    res ispa loquitur 20–1
  standard of care 11–19
    children 15
    cost and practicability of precautions 18–19
    definition 11–12
    foreseen by reasonable person 19
    likelihood of injury 17
    magnitude of risk 17–18
    medical negligence 13–14
    reasonable person 12
    seriousnes of injury 18
    skilled or professional defendants 13
    social value of defendants' activities 19
    special 12–16
    sporting events 16
    unskilled defendants 14–15

causation and negligence 26, 27–34
  factual causation 27–31
    but for test 27–8
    "novus actus interveniens" 31–4
      act of claimant 33
      act of nature 34
      third party act 32–3
    proving – problems in 28–31
      lost
        chance cases 30–1
        multiple causes of damage 28–30
        multiple consecutive causes of damage 31

children
  and contributory negligence 155–6
  liability in negligence 15
  as visitors 88–9

coastguard, duty of care 10

consent as defence see defences – general, consent

contributory negligence

as defence
  to occupiers' liability 92
  see also under defences- general

damages 163–9
  aggravated 166–7
    compared with exemplary 167–8
  contemptuous 166
  exemplary 166–7
    compared with aggravated 167–8
  general 166
  loss of earnings 166
  medical expenses 166
  mitigation of loss 165
  nominal 166
  for personal injury 168
  special 166

defamation 135–46
  availability 138
  defences 141–3
    consent 142
    fair comment 142
    innocent publication 141
    justification 142
    offer of amends 143
    privilege 141, 142
  elements 138–41
    defamatory statement 139–40
    definition 139
    publication of statement 141
    statement must refer to claimant 140–1
  privacy or freedom of expression 144
  remedies 143–4
    damages 143
    injunction 143–4

right to trial by jury 138
slander compared with libel
137–8
time limit for claims 138
defences – general 147–59
consent – *volenti non fit
injuria* 92, 149–52
consent of claimant 151–2
employees 151
participants and
spectators 152
passengers in vehicles
151
knowledge of risk 150–1
contributory negligence 154–9
apportionment of blame
157–9
children 155–6
claimant's damage 154
claimant's fault 154–5
emergency situations 157
rescuers 157
standard of care 155–7
illegality *ex turpi causa non
oritur actio* 152–4
defences – specific
list of 159
see also relevant tort

economic loss, and negligence
see negligence,
economic loss
egg-shell skull rule 36–7
and psychiatric injury 51
emergency situations, and
contributory
negligence 157
employee
and consent to harm 151
determination of status 57–60
control test 57–8
economic reality test 58–60
organisation or integration
test 58
employer/employee relationship,
duty of care 8
employers' liability 68–81
common law duty 70–4
competent duty 74
non-delegable duty 70
safe equipment 72
safe premises 71

safe system of work 72
statutory duty – breach of
74–9
courts determination of
right of action in tort
75–6
defences 78–9
consent 79
contributory negligence
79
elements of tort (if statute
allows civil claim)
76–8
breach of duty by
defendant 77
causation 78
damage 78
statutory duty owed to
claimant 76–7
ex turpi causa non oritur actio
152–4

false imprisonment 128–30
defences 129–30
lawful arrest 130
medical detention 130
reasonable condition for
release 129–30
definition 128
knowledge of constraint 129
partial constraint 129
total loss of freedom 128–9
fire service, duty of care 10
foreseeability of harm, and
contributory
negligence 155
freedom of expression 144

harassment 131–2

independent contractors, and
occupiers' liability
91–2
injunctions 169–72
definition 169
and equitable remedies 172
final 172
interim (interlocutory) 171–2
mandatory 169
prohibitory 169
quia timet 170–1
injuries

and contributory negligence,
reductions in damages
158
damages for 168
injuries in workplace
number of 69
see also employers' liability
interim injunction 171–2
interlocutory injunction 171

joint liability, definition 65

libel
basis of damages 138
compared with slander 137–8
see also defamation

medical detention, as defence for
false imprisonment
130
medical negligence, standard of
care 13–14

negligence 1–53
breach of duty *see* breach of
duty and negligence
causation *see* causation and
negligence
definition 4
legal definition compared
with everyday usage 2
duty of care 4–10
basic elements in
establishing –
summary 8
established duty situations
5
liability for failing to act 7–9
exceptions 7–8
neighbour principle 5–7
special protection 9–10
unborn children 9
economic loss 4, 41–4
acquisition of defective
goods or property
43–4
damage to property 42–3
definition 41
establishing, procedure when
answering questions
3
psychiatric injury *see*

psychiatric injury,
liability for
remoteness 34–7
egg-shell skull rule 36–7
test of 34–6
special duties 40–53
see also negligent
misstatement
negligent misstatement 40, 44–6
liability to third parties 46
special relationship
requirement 45–6
"novus actus interveniens" 31–4
nuisance 96–111
defences 107–9
effective defences 107–8
prescription 107–8
statutory authority 108
ineffective defences 108–9
actions of others 109
coming to the nuisance
109
public benefit 109
private nuisance 97, 98–103
damage 104
definition 98
forms 98–9
rights and interests in
property 99–100
unreasonable use of land
101–3
character of
neighbourhood 101
duration of nuisance 102
malice 103
public benefit 103
sensitivity ofclaimant
101–2
public nuisance 97, 104–7
class of people 104–6
definition 104
special damage 106–7
remedies 109–10
abatement 110
damages and injunctions
109–10

occupier/visitor relationship, duty
of care 8
occupiers' liability 82–95
1957 Act 83, 84–92
defences 92

contributory negligence
92
use of notices 92
"violenti non fit injuria"
92
duty of care 87–90
children 88–9
skiled visitors 90
independent contractors
91–2
premises, definition 85–6
purpose of Act 85
visitors – categories 86–7
with express permission
86
with implied permission
86–7
with right to enter 87
warning signs 90–1
1984 Act 83, 92–4
duty of care 93
signs and defences 94
trespasser, definition 93
definition of occupier 85

parent/child relationship, duty of
care 8
parental authority, as defence to
assault and battery
127
passengers in vehicles, and
consent to harm 151
police, duty of care 9
prison officers/prisoner
relationship, duty of
care 7
privacy 144
psychiatric injury, liability for 40,
41, 47–51
definition 47–8
duty of care 58–0
primary victims 49–50
reasonably foreseeable
victim 49–50
secondary victims 49, 50
egg-shell skull rule 51
proximity 50
remoteness 51
public authorities, duty of care
10

quia timet injunction 170–1

remedies 162–74
damages *see separate entry*
injunctions *see separate entry*
res ispa loquitur 20–1
rescuers, and contributory
negligence 157

seatbelts, failure to wear,
reductions in damages
158
self-defence, as defence to
assault and battery 127
several liability, definition 65
slander
basis of damages 138
compared with libel 137–8
see also defamation
sporting events
breach of duty and
negligence, standard of
care 16
participants and spectators,
and consent to harm
152

trespass to land 112–19
airspace 116–17
defences 118
consent 118
contractual licence 118
defences 118
lawful authority 118
definition 114
elements of 114–16
awareness of trespass 115
direct interference 114–15
no harm or damage 115
voluntary interference 115
manisfestations 116–17
meaning of land 116–17
protected interests 117
remedies 118
possession orders 118
self-help 118
trespass *ab initio* 117
trespass to the person 120–34
assault *see separate entry*
battery *see separate entry*
defences 132
false imprisonment *see
separate entry*
harassment 131–2

indirect harm (*Wilkinson v Downton*) 130–1
trespasser, definition 93

unborn children, duty of care 9

vicarious liability 54–67
  in course of employment 60–4
    acts beyond the scope of employment 62
    authorised acts 61

authorised acts in unauthorised manner 61–2
employee, determination of status *see separate entry*
express prohibitions 62–3
intentional wrongful acts 63–4
definition 55
employer's indemnity 64–5

Civil Liability (Contribution) Act 64–5
  common law indemnity 65
  essential components 56–7
  examples of relationships 56
  tort commited 60
"violenti non fit injuria" 92

warning signs, and occupiers' liability 90–1